Nobody does

FAST TRACK
to the
CORNER OFFICE
for WOMEN

Second Edition

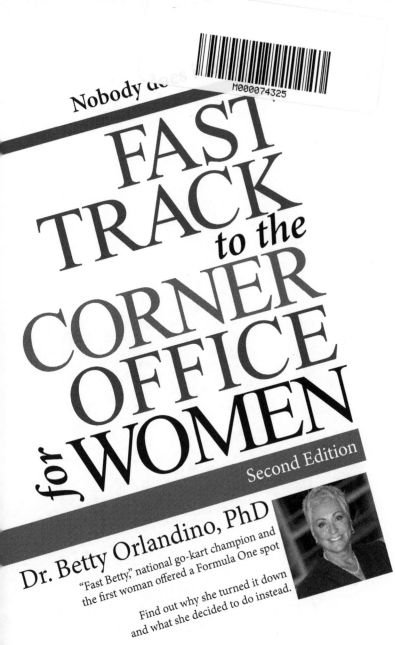

Dr. Betty Orlandino, PhD

"Fast Betty," national go-kart champion and
the first woman offered a Formula One spot

Find out why she turned it down
and what she decided to do instead.

BRADFORD JEWELL Publishing

Published by: Bradford Jewell Publishing

For more information, contact: Dr.Betty@DrBettyO.com

Printed: April 2019

ISBN: 978-1-7336869-0-7 (paperback)

ISBN: 978-1-7336869-1-4 (e-book)

Cover design by: Layne Mitchell

Interior design: Patrizia Sceppa, Inc.

Printed in the United States of America

Fast Track to the Corner Office for Women
by Dr. Betty Orlandino, PhD

This book is dedicated to mentors near and far, who generously provided their time, experience, and wisdom with no obligation, other than the simple expectation to "pay it forward." And to my family of clients, who teach me something new about people every day we work together, God bless you one and all.

"Fast Betty," national go-kart champion and the first woman offered a Formula One spot, in 1968.

Find out why she turned it down and what she decided to do instead.

Contents

Quotes from Amazing Women

"You think about what would have happened . . .
Suppose I had gotten a job as a permanent associate.
Probably I would have climbed the ladder and today
I would be a retired partner. So often in life, things
that you regard as an impediment turn out to be
great good fortune." *—Ruth Bader Ginsburg*

"Surround yourself only with people who will take
you higher." *—Oprah Winfrey*

"Success isn't about how much money you make. It's
about the difference you make in people's lives."
—Michelle Obama

"Life is about creating new opportunities, not waiting
for them to come to you." *—Salma Hayek*

"Make bold choices and make mistakes." *—Angelina Jolie*

"We need to tell each other our stories."
—Jennifer Lawrence

"It took me quite a long time to find a voice, and
now that I have it, I am not going to be silent."
—Madeleine Albright

"Taking initiative pays off. It is hard to visualize
someone as a leader if she is always waiting to be
told what to do." *—Sheryl Sandberg*

Foreword

If you are a young woman just graduating college or a gainfully employed female who wants her seat at the corporate table, this book is for you. This book was written to provide women with a jump-start to their career, to help give them an equal shot at the "corner office" and show them how to move on to the C-suite.

Let's really be honest—the playing field is not fair. And though it has improved significantly in the last fifty years, it is still far from being level.

I know it as a daughter who watched my own mom blaze a path for other women her entire life, yet never achieve the recognition or status she earned. I know it as a woman who has toughed it out for the past sixty-six years, including over thirty years with insider "VIP executive access" as a coach and mentor to corporate America's top men and women in business. And I know it as a mother, observing the battle my own daughter fights every day to ensure her continued success in the technically and emotionally demanding career she's chosen.

In short, I hear stories every day about young women who are not treated with dignity and respect. Women who are still trying to get due recognition and rewards for their stellar work and achievements.

That's why I believe the battle for equal opportunity and equal pay for women is far from over today. It's why I am committed to make certain that we close that gap of inequality, as quickly and surely as we can.

I've known for years that my legacy is to help women to have their fair shot at achieving their goals.

. . by sharing the wisdom of my mentors, my own real-world experience as a woman with my own family and my own business, and my proven track record with over thirty years of successes as a coach, mentor, and entrepreneur.

Today's competition is fierce—more so than ever before. We are not only competing across America with the largest pool of educated candidates in history. With the technology revolution currently and constantly happening all around us, we are now also competing globally.

Fast Track to the Corner Office for Women has only one agenda: to help women navigate their career trajectory and achieve their goals without unnecessary roughness, drama, or delay.

Remember: as women, we have unique gifts we need to tap into. And as you'll see in the case studies discussed throughout this book, our greatest gift is our women's intuition. So use it, in combination with your innate abilities to listen, to extrapolate, and to read body language.

While you're at it, employ your endless patience, your unlimited resourcefulness, and your innate tolerance for pain to your advantage. Nobody does it better than a single mom, so stop thinking single moms are at a disadvantage—they are a breed of their own.

In real life, competencies can always be learned. More important, women are innately strong, and take adversity and conflict in stride. For example, have you ever seen a mom stay in bed all day when she is sick, when she has an infant or children that need to be cared for? Most of the women I've known usually don't get a real day off, as they use their time to organize, clean, catch up on errands, shop for groceries, etc. Believe me, we're not exactly sitting around eating bonbons!

Acknowledge and appreciate your inherent strengths for what they really are: tremendous advantages. If you're not using them, your spark plugs are misfiring.

You know, as women, our insights into pain tolerance give us an unexpected inside track to achievement, even wisdom. If we stayed home every time we weren't feeling well, the world would be in big trouble! Your patience and tolerance for pain gives you stamina and unrelenting strength. And your intuition gives you the master plan to use your strengths to the max, one day at a time.

In fact, just as I was finishing up my notes for this book, I was struck by the number of times I've let my intuition guide me in some major decisions during my life. The connections that came about as a result have been mind-boggling. There's no way I could have masterminded them all on my own, but looking back on things now, I've seen how they all fell into place to bring me to where I am today. As you read through the chapters here, think about how intuition has helped guide your decisions too.

It's time to reframe your thinking about how your womanhood might be a disadvantage. Instead, recognize the clear advantage it actually is for you. To get started, step into your confidence, put on your big-girl skirt, and begin by memorizing the *Ten Steps to Fast Track Your Way to the Corner Office*. Ladies, start your engines please.

–Dr. Betty O

Ten Steps to Fast-Track Your Way to the Corner Office

1. Find a **mentor** and a **coach**.

2. Recognize that **politics** are as important as **performance**.

3. Establish your **brand**.

4. Do your **homework** on the organization or your competitors.

5. Focus on **building a coalition**.

6. Reinvigorate your **optimism** and **positive self-talk**.

7. Develop excellent **communication** and **people skills**.

8. Demonstrate an **excellent work ethic**.

9. Expand and utilize your **network** to serve your **community**.

10. Live with **passion** and respond with **compassion**.

Introduction

I was compelled to write this book in memory of my mother, Helen Weber, who helped pave the way for me and generations of other women to have their voices heard—because the real silent majority is female.

My mother worked tirelessly as a nurse for forty-three years, only to pass away six months after she retired. I remember our family actually received a letter from President Ronald Reagan the following year, thanking her for her service to her country. Unfortunately, the honor arrived a year too late.

I wrote this book because I do not want my daughter, granddaughters, nieces, or any other woman to have to struggle needlessly, and to lower their self-confidence as a direct result.

Of course, no one's journey is without obstacles, but most women experience more discouragement, pain, and frustration along the way than any man could imagine. As women, we are often operating with conflicting messages: have a career, have children. Why are you working? Or why, as a parent, aren't you working too?

Although it wasn't always this way, today we can choose the life we want to lead. In fact, I had to choose between a career in racing or raising a family in the sixties. Yes, for women, things have improved some, but don't be fooled—it is still not an equal playing field. If you think it is, you are either a man, or you are kidding yourself.

Back in the day, women's choices were so extremely limited. And that is why I want to help give women their fair shot at success and happiness, by providing insights, exposing lies we have been told, and unveiling the truths we must be aware of.

This book is written by a woman, for women. And in the same ways the women who have mentored, guided, and shaped my life have helped me find my own fast track to success, I'll use short descriptions, actual examples, and real-life stories to show you what works in the real world.

CHAPTER 1

"Where There's a Will..."

I grew up in Park Ridge, Illinois, a suburb of Chicago. As a young girl, I noticed my mom (a nurse) was the only working mom in the entire neighborhood. This was 1955, and women were still expected to stay at home and care for their families. That was the assigned role for women in those days. Meanwhile, my dad owned a Sinclair gas station.

So, with both of my parents working very long hours, my German grandmother (a mighty tough lady) raised me and my sister, Lynne. My sister was typically in very poor health and was five years older than me.

In hindsight, my early life prepared me very well for the hardships and disappointments experienced by the majority of women. At the time, I did not see any advantage to being reminded every day by my grandmother about what a curse it was to be a woman and how cumbersome it was to raise a family.

To be fair, Grandma Sophie had it hard, as did all of the dirt-poor, immigrant farmers in the late 1800s and early 1900s. No electricity, no running water—*no* seemed to be the operative word for just about everything.

I guess it is no wonder my grandma was so bitter and unhappy. Sophie was one of nine children living on the family farm in Pontiac, Illinois. They survived on bread and milk six days a week, and on Sundays, they killed two chickens for the entire family's meal. At Christmas, each child received an apple or an orange, as Kris Kringle never paid a visit to their farm.

As a young girl, Sophie loved going to school, but she was forced to quit during the winter of second grade to help the family survive. She got a job scrubbing floors on her hands and knees six days a week at the only hotel in town.

She was seven years old!

Life never seemed fair, and never seemed to get any easier for little Sophie. Her brothers got to go to school—mind you, they worked before and after classes, feeding the chickens, milking the cows, and working the fields. But girls didn't need schoolin', as everyone knew they would be cooking, sewing, and caring for their family. That was their lot in life.

At age eighteen, Sophie married Roy Weber. They started their own farm and began to raise their own family. My mother, Helen, was their only child, born in 1914. For the next ten years, they worked, ate, prayed, and slept. That is about all that time permitted in those days.

When Helen was ten years old, Roy developed a very severe case of tonsillitis. He would not see a doctor, because the farm duties could not wait—and because it cost money (although in those days, doctors were often paid with chickens, eggs, and dairy, or some other type of in-kind payment).

Roy died two weeks later, as the infection spread to his heart. He was twenty-nine years old.

As you can imagine, Sophie was not only grieving, but now she was a single mom on a farm, left to work the fields, manage the livestock, cook, clean, and raise a daughter by herself. She was twenty-eight years old and could barely read or write.

In subsequent years, Sophie became literate. Her German was better than her English, but she was determined to become fluent in English too. And she did.

Sophie was so very lonely and scared, but nevertheless determined to do whatever it took to survive and raise her daughter. There were no appliances, no phones, and no neighbors within walking distance. It was dark when she got up in the morning, and dark when she finally put her head on the pillow at night. In Pontiac, she was known as "The Widow Weber," and she rolled up her sleeves and managed to save the farm.

It's hard to imagine the fortitude and commitment required to live under those circumstances. But with her strong will and determination, Sophie learned carpentry, plumbing, farming, and repairs, as she only had herself to count on.

She was real, living proof that where there is a will, there is a way.

My mom Helen grew up in the small town of Pontiac, Illinois, at a time when the career choices were farming or working at the Pontiac prison.

Helen already felt like she was in prison, and she was determined to not stay in Pontiac. So, at eighteen years of age, she got out of Dodge by bus and arrived in Evanston, Illinois. She stayed with a cousin there and put herself through nursing school at Evanston Hospital (a prestigious institution in its time, and the forerunner of today's Northwestern Memorial Hospital).

Graduating at the top of her class, my mom was immediately hired as a registered nurse at Evanston Hospital. She continued to work as a nurse until Pearl Harbor Day (December 7, 1941). Not surprisingly, on December 8, 1941, like scores of other patriots, my mom enlisted in the US Army Medical Corps. She served overseas (North Africa and European campaigns) until the end of the war.

Looking back, I know my mom Helen was way ahead of her time. She was decisive and took action, regardless of being discouraged by so many of the people around her simply because she was a woman.

My mom, Lt. Helen M. Weber, RN, a woman who was years ahead of her time!

COULD YOU WAKE UP IN TIME TO SAVE YOUR OWN LIFE?

Back home in the United States in 1946, my mom suddenly became ill. She was admitted to Evanston Hospital in intensive care, with a raging fever and in a coma. The medical team was at a loss. Throughout her treatment, they repeatedly said, "We are losing her!"

After two days and seemingly on her deathbed, my mom came out of her coma long enough to say a single word: "Malaria."

The doctors and nurses were perplexed—malaria in Evanston, Illinois? They were about to dismiss the comment when one of the nurses recalled that my mom served overseas, as the head nurse for the US Army Medical Research Project on Malaria.

Yes, my mom saved her own life! Once again, she was counting on herself, as she always had. She was outspoken, self-reliant and not always popular, but she got the job done . . . and she saved countless lives, even her own.

Packing in the double shifts for the next forty-three years, she continued her nursing career, rising to the top of the ranks. I know she instilled a work ethic in me, not just by words, but by her actions. My mom made the world a better place.

In a strange way, my family history made me the woman I am today too. You see, because my sister Lynne had major health issues as a child that continued all of her life, my grandmother favored her.

I admit, as a little girl, it hurt me a great deal to be dismissed or shushed so as not to bother my sister. But eventually, with my mother and grandmother as role models, it forced me to become self-reliant and fiercely independent, and to avoid looking to others for my own outcomes. I certainly was not the typical baby of the family, and actually became a caregiver very early on. I was going to make a difference in this world, and nobody was going to stop me, even though I was a girl!

In fact, my grandmother didn't know it, but hearing her tell me "girls can't do that" so many times actually provided the motivation for me to prove her wrong. I've got to thank Granny Sophie for that!

The point is, we can take any message, even a discouraging one, and use it to our advantage. We can also elect to use it as an excuse to not achieve our goals or succeed. That was never an option for me, and you should not let it be an option for you.

Now that I have a daughter of my own, she inspires me to help other women. I saw how hard Jacki had to fight to earn her place at the top of a technically and emotionally challenging profession: forensic toxicology. She continues to deal with biases and prejudices on a daily basis too.

My daughter Jacki, graduating with high honors as a forensic toxicologist

CHAPTER 2

Why Do I Need a Mentor? Good Luck Without One!

As a Certified Talent Consultant and Master Performance Coach, I work with Fortune 100 and Fortune 500 executives and their teams to make them the best that they can possibly be—to empower them with leadership, communication, and other skills in order to achieve their goals.

I help people to discover and overcome the road-blocks along the way . . . especially the barriers that are hiding in plain sight. My clients are celebrities, professional athletes, C-suite executives, and female entrepreneurs, who need a mentor and coach they can trust. For insights, behavioral change, growth and personal accountability in the increasingly competitive cut-throat world of today, they call me.

My clients get the benefit of 550 years of experience. Just how is that possible? Personally I have 40 years of experience in business, along with a PhD in psychology and a generous helping of common sense. But I also carry the collective wisdom of all of my mentors and coaches, as you will read in the stories I am about to share. And as you'll discover in the chapters in this book, each of my mentors had 50 years or more of their own experience to share, rising to great heights in their own business and social circles.

In short, their experience became mine. And so did their networks, contacts, and connections. That's how it works, if you are doing this right. Just remember that one of the best ways to accelerate your career or knowledge is by "standing on the shoulders of giants." Learn from the experience of mentors. Ask questions. Pay attention to their answers and their actions. Let them help you figure out the things you need to know, to go places they've already been. Don't rely on trial and error—that is the slow and painful way!

WHAT IS THE DIFFERENCE BETWEEN A COACH AND A MENTOR?

A coach helps you develop specific skill sets, usually based on a particular project or career move. To put it simply, coaching creates skills mastery. A mentor is a loyal friend and advisor. She sees you not as you are, but who you could be. A mentor builds on strengths and helps to shore up weaknesses. Mentoring develops the whole person, fostering the gathering of wisdom and experience in the "real" world. Mentors also share their networks and connections to help mentees establish themselves in their careers.

If you are operating without a coach and a mentor, you are at a disadvantage.

WHY WOULD A C-SUITE EXECUTIVE OR SUPERSTAR NEED A COACH?

Because they know that nobody does it alone. The biggest (and longest lasting) Grammy-winning and Oscar-winning celebs, CEOs, and professional athletes all have someone they can trust to coach and mentor them.

We all need a safe place and a trusted confidant to help us fast track, strategize business decisions, fine-tune our career paths, and secure our legacy.

Let me ask you a question: Who's got your back?

Your answer might be your spouse, your best friend, your mom or dad, or a colleague. And they may in fact be someone you can trust too, but how objective are they really?

A performance coach's only agenda is your success and happiness. After all, your spouse may mean well, but they may have only a limited real understanding of the business you are in, as well as a natural bias toward you.

In a similar way, your colleagues have their own career to think of. And more often than you might think, they'll avoid bringing up a subject that's uncomfortable or "goes against the grain," especially when it's something you're doing, not them.

So who really has your back? If you are a woman, you can really feel alone and vulnerable in the world, especially the corporate world!

SELECTING MENTORS AND COACHES

Mentors must be carefully selected, as they are a key to your success and happiness. For a mentoring relationship to work, the mentor's only agenda must be to provide wisdom and guidance to you. They must be willing to tell you the truth, pointing out your blind spots with candor in order for you to course-correct in real time. Mentors do not have to be in the same field or occupation or have the same interests. They simply need to have your back and be truthful.

In most cases, it is best to select someone significantly more experienced than you are, to assure there is no direct competition or conflict of interest. Also, choose someone who has already succeeded in the areas you want to learn about. They also need to have time to provide you with counsel without taking away from their own needs. Ideally, have at least two mentors on your roster, and open yourself to female and male perspectives. When selecting a coach, find one with real experience in the business arena, not just academics and theories. And remember, your mentor must have common sense; it is as valuable as their experience and mental prowess. Emotional intelligence will also often take you further than a formal education.

The right fit is crucial to the success of the coaching relationship. If the coach and the client cannot relate, it doesn't matter how qualified or impressive the coach is. After all, coaching and mentoring are very intimate relationships built on the participants connecting with absolute trust.

I recommend interviewing several coaches, in real-life scenarios if at all possible. Trust your gut as to which one feels right. Do not just look at a resume or their LinkedIn page, since someone else may have written it for them. Meet the real person first. If they don't have time to talk to you before charging you, you might want to think twice.

Again, don't limit yourself to one mentor or one coach. Everyone has something to teach, even if it is what not to do. I have had a dozen different mentors over the years and expect there will be someone else in the wings going forward. I have been mentored by men, women, graduate students, and multimillion-dollar-business owners. Some of my mentors never had a job, but were married to billionaires and provided another perspective on life and social skills.

OPPORTUNITIES FOR MENTORSHIP

The best part is, opportunities for mentorship can come anytime or anywhere. So hold an idea in the back of your mind of what you want to develop in yourself or what you need, then let the best mentors for you show up. When they arrive, trust your instincts and reach out. Ask for what you want. You must take action and be proactive.

Share your expertise or interest by mentoring, and you will draw wonderful people to yourself.

Marilyn Jacobson, PhD, a professor at Loyola University in Chicago, was so generous and helpful to me over the years. Even though we met when we were both consulting at the same company, she took it upon herself to help me with my coaching assignments when I went back to school for postgraduate training. My formal education included a master's in social work and a PhD in psychology. Fortunately, Marilyn helped me to understand the academics of the MBA program. Marilyn was a professor in the MBA program at Loyola; it was like getting the Cliff's Notes to an MBA program while I was working. The most valuable lesson I learned from her was that you don't have to know everything about everything, as you can learn about things on demand.

As anyone who knows me will tell you, I am always saying "Go to school on everyone!" It has become my mantra, and it serves as a reminder that you can learn from a wide range of mentors, not just the good ones, but also the ones that end up showing you what not to do.

I had an invaluable mentor early in my consulting career, a coach whose name I shall not reveal. This man does not know it, but he provided me with one of the best lessons of all. I watched him lose clients time and time again, simply by letting his ego get in the way. Instead of explaining to his clients another way to approach a problem, he would berate and insult them. I realized that if I did just the opposite, I could be very successful. If I saw a situation going sideways, I would gently lead clients to find another solution. I learned what not to do from him—equally as valuable as learning what to do.

Your big takeaway here is to go to school on everyone: it is free, and in the worst case, you will learn what not to do.

I remember a senator, another of my most influential mentors, acting like a complete jerk one day. I was so embarrassed. He took me out for lunch and while we were in this trendy restaurant, he literally was snapping his fingers at the busboy and the waiter. Apparently, he'd been insulted when the service he was receiving wasn't up to the imagined standards he felt he deserved. He kept saying, "Do you know who I am?"

For years a senator had been so generous with his advice to me, but that day I saw a side of him that I had never seen before. I made the decision to never go out to eat with him again after witnessing his rudeness and abuse of his perceived power. We remained friends, and I will always be grateful for the lessons he shared, including this lesson of how not to behave.

Here is one more example of going to school on everyone. While I was working as a teacher in elementary school, I had the pleasure of taking a kindergarten class to gym for some fun.

As a teacher, I always wanted to pose challenges as questions to solve, to make learning more interesting and engaging. Setting up the relay races with four-wheeled scooters, I said to the children "Take your scooter to the other end of the gym as fast as you can and back, then sit down cross-legged."

In a flurry of activity, I watched as some little ones laid on their bellies on the scooters and struggled, some went on their knees and found they could go even faster, and some found if you went backwards you really could go super fast. I then noticed a little red-haired boy pick his scooter up and run with it in his hands. I laughed so hard. It goes to show you, anyone can teach you something, even a little child. Don't assume only experience, age, and education provide value!

I want to see you raise your hand and find your voice from day one. Believe me, you want to create the perception that will serve you best. It is not who you are, but who you are perceived to be, that will follow you throughout your career.

Dr. Betty and Tony-winning Broadway legend Rachel Bay Jones

Betty O at a friend's wedding, with Judge Judy, Florence Henderson, and Barry Manilow

As you read the professional anecdotes and very personal stories scattered throughout this book, you'll encounter a handful of incredible personalities I've known who rose to heights in their career and social life that most people would love to aspire to.

They did it even though they often asked themselves the same questions you probably have when your gut tells you something you don't want to hear. You know, things like "Oh shoot, this relationship isn't working," or "I need to quit my job," or "I need to get a divorce."

I ask those questions too—all the time. And sometimes, when the right answer comes up, I don't want to hear it. I fight it. And I put off making a choice that I know would actually help me in a heartbeat.

But as you'll see, some of the best situations came out of trusting my mentor's advice, and then acting on my best instincts. Outcomes I couldn't have predicted if I tried.

CHAPTER 3

Girls Can't
Do That

I was an exceptional athlete in school, but that was before Title IX took effect. It seemed that whatever I was interested in was encouraged for boys but dismissed for girls.

At the same time, I loved mechanics and making things, probably from my experiences at my dad's gas station shop. In fact, I petitioned to be included in shop classes at Maine South High School. (Yes, I sat next to Hillary Clinton in study hall; she was one class ahead of me. You know, she was ambitious and driven and knew what she wanted even back then. While the rest of us were having fun, she was studying and strategizing.)

Anyway, the petition to let me into shop classes was declined—even though I was the state champion in go-karting at the time, on my way to becoming national champion. It seemed those events were reminding me: hope was only offered to the boys.

Didn't stop me, though. Here's the story.

In 1960, a go-kart track named Evans International Raceway was built about five miles from my home. My parents didn't want me to race (because I was a girl), but I was determined to be a driver. So I went for it, even at eleven years old. I practically ran away from home to go racing! I'd ride my bike there every day after school, because they offered rental cards at fifty cents for three laps—and on Wednesdays and Sundays, they held races.

After two months of working for free on the rentals (so I could get free rides), the owner of the track told me he had been watching me, and that I was very skilled with the karts. He asked if I would like to enter a race with his kart in the junior class the next weekend.

Are you kidding? I was in heaven! I won that race, and by the time my parents discovered what was happening, I had already won a championship. I was hooked.

Fortunately, my mom and dad realized how much I loved racing and found the funds so that I could continue. Within a few more months, I became the first female member of a prestigious racing team at Evans International. And at only twelve years of age, I soon learned the power of mentoring and relationships.

The next few years brought me spectacular learning experiences, on and off the track. I became the national champion and won races all over the country, with my final victory at the New York World's Fair in 1965.

Even then, something told me I was helping to turn the tide for women. When I turned eighteen, I was the very first female offered a Formula One spot ever.

Believe it or not, I turned it down, because I wanted a family and an education—decisions men don't have to consider. It was the toughest decision of my life at the time and remains one of the pivotal moments of my life even now, all these years later.

You see, during my career in racing, I learned some of the most important life lessons, many of which apply to the business world too. It turns out that the men were very unhappy about being beaten by a woman. And most of them were very ego-driven. I witnessed and experienced lying, cheating, sabotaged equipment, equipment theft, and a host of other disgusting behaviors directed towards me.

That's when I learned that the world isn't exactly fair. Women are indeed treated differently. The boys, club existed then, and it still does today.

Don't get me wrong—I am grateful for every one of those experiences, as they got me ready for the real world and life. At eighteen years of age, I was way ahead of the game.

I also met a few wonderful men who were gracious, generous, and encouraging, like Wally Strange, who owned the Evans International Raceway and gave me my first break. That's when I first learned not to go it alone.

My first experience with mentoring came through my racing, and has become an invaluable key to my life and success. God bless all of the mentors I have had and will have going forward.

My life was about to do another 180-degree turn, in ways I'd never imagined.

CHAPTER 4

Shifting Gears

Behind the wheel of championship racing karts all across the country, I was in my glory–and my own personal heaven.

However, as a young woman, I knew I wanted a family, so I decided to shift my priorities and get out of racing. Besides, I was getting tired of a few unsavory characters in the biz at the time, plus the demanding schedules and nonstop, cross-country touring, always in a different town, a different state, a different racing course.

A couple of years later, I got married on the Fourth of July, at age twenty-one. In my mind–and in the social context of the mid-1960s–it was the right thing for a young woman to do. The wedding itself was an eye-opener for me, with guest after guest coming up to my new father-in-law to give him $100 to $500 cash gifts for his son's wedding, just like that scene in the movie *The Godfather*!

One thing I was very certain of–given my history, I was going to get an education and make a difference in the world.

I poured my heart and all my creativity into my studies at the University of Illinois, taking on extra coursework and earning extra course credit for study-hall hours as a teacher's aide. True to my nickname, Fast Betty, I graduated in only three years and was proudly on the dean's list every semester.

Applying my college credentials immediately, I soon qualified to work as a teacher in the Oak Park School District. But after teaching in the school system for about five years, I realized I was doing more counseling than the school counselors. Even the principal relied on my rapport to work with children who were having difficulties.

That is when I began my quest for a master's degree to become a therapist. In truth, I still loved teaching, but found my experiences counseling the children were the best part of my job. I continued to work at the school for six more years, as completing my graduate program part-time in the evenings and on Saturdays was a long haul.

Of course, I needed to have my income, as well as the stipend I received for working with student teachers in my classroom.

Before I took over as the gym-class instructor for some of the younger grades at Oak Park, children with disabilities were not allowed to take part in athletics. It was apparently a huge mind-shift for most people to think of allowing them to participate too. For some reason, those in charge had assumed these kids couldn't do anything.

Yes, they can.

Even the kids in the wheelchairs would have skates on, and they could go home and proudly say they had skated. Yes, they were in their wheelchair—so what? They had skates on! Their rollers were touching the ground.

It was beautiful to see. Because it's all about making people feel good about themselves and building their confidence to empower them to do what they can do.

Those kids had more gumption than anybody I ever saw. For some of them, it took an hour and a half in the morning to get their braces on before the special bus would even pick them up to take them to school. And I realized that those are the kids who are smiling all the time!

They were so grateful to be able to participate in anything. I'd take them on the balance beam, and I'd be holding them on it, but they could say they were on the beam doing gymnastics. And I'd have the newspapers come and take pictures of them, and they'd get their name in the paper.

Can you imagine? What a thrill! They were getting support and attention like they'd never had before. They felt normal for a day.

They felt special, because they did it!

That became my philosophy of coaching. Its purpose is to bring out the best in someone. Everybody's got problems, but why focus on those? Build on your strengths and find that special piece that makes you feel unstoppable.

Fortunately, I found a way to return to grad school on a stipend, supplementing my income by supervising student teachers at the school. That meant I could have all my tuition paid with no money out of pocket while I was at university. I was thrilled!

The day I came home and announced that I had found a way to attend grad school for free, I was so excited and proud of my resourcefulness.

Betty O teaching gym class in Oak Park, Illinois

Unfortunately, that day also signaled the end of my seven-year marriage. Our interests were changing as rapidly as my young daughter was growing up. It was nobody's fault; my husband and I simply wanted different things out of life. We were just on different pages.

After working my way through school for the six years after my divorce, I graduated from the University of Illinois at Chicago Circle (UICC) with high honors in 1981, then opened my practice six months later and never looked back. Within a few years, I was making a name for myself, and had four offices throughout the Chicago area.

Starting out, I paid a nominal $100 fee for part-time "Wednesday plus weekends" usage of my first office for the entire month. I shared the space with other like-minded professionals on their days off and after hours (including chiropractors, fertility specialists, acupuncturists, etc.), and we all made cross-referrals to each other's practices. Along the way, I was careful to select prestigious doctors, so my name was associated with their good brand.

Within six months, I had a booming practice. Over the next three years, I duplicated the recipe by opening three more offices (covering the north, south, east and west regions of Chicago. This strategy helped me draw from a larger area, so as to always have an active stream of business coming in to my practice.

My reputation in the industry grew in stature and notoriety during the early eighties (partly thanks to a few noteworthy projects), and I was appearing in news media and television interviews quite a lot. Before long, my associates were benefitting from my name on the door at all four offices. We still continued to share referrals, so I had no out-of-pocket expenses for office rent for years.

In other words, I was time-sharing the office space I needed, adding to those resources as my business warranted it. As they say, "Necessity is the mother of invention." (Notice how the saying isn't "father of invention.")

In the same way, you can always be on the lookout for ways to get what you want by being resourceful. See, I didn't have the money to pay for one office, let alone four! But I quickly had my name on the door, and it's very impressive to have four offices.

In fact, one of them was in Water Tower Place, and that was the building in downtown Chicago. It still is. I had an office there for fifteen years, and I never paid a dime for it!

That's the awesome power of being resourceful. Get smart. Negotiate an exchange where both sides win. Find a way to make it work. Remember, if you're going about it the same way other people are doing things, at best, you're going to end up with the same results.

Want something different? Then do something different!

The first year I launched my practice, I published my first book, *Infertility Counseling and Psychotherapy,* as an authoritative platform for creating awareness of the problem and of my unique position as the premier solution provider in the industry.

In addition, I gave free talks at community centers, chambers of commerce–anywhere I could. Then I would write press releases, advertising and following up with local papers to get my name out there. I contacted the news assignment editors at TV and radio stations and made myself available for interviews. After all, if people read about you, hear you on radio, or see you on television, you must be the expert!

And that's exactly how it worked out. When the editors at *Time* magazine were looking for someone to interview for a feature on infertility, they couldn't help noticing my presence in the industry. Finally, on September 10, 1984, my interview appeared in *Time,* exploding my popularity and my practice even further.

Betty O with daughter Jacki, 1983

In short, I loved my life. My daughter was my absolute joy. My practice was gratifying, and I was changing people's lives for the better. My family was healthy, and I had just been accepted to a PhD program in psychology.

What more could anyone ask for?

Unexpectedly, I received a phone call in 1991 from a psychologist friend who owned a business consulting firm. He asked me to join his group of associates.

At first, I was confused about how I'd fit in, as I was a trained therapist. He explained to me that I was perfect for the job because I was engaging, loved people, was a great communicator, and always brought out the best in others.

I was flattered, but not convinced. So my friend asked me to take on one assignment, just to see if I would like it. I agreed to give it a try, as the assignment was very exciting and lucrative.

As it turned out, I didn't like it—I loved it! But I was in a quandary, as I also loved being a therapist. So, I decided I would take on only those business consulting assignments that I had great interest in, just as I did in my psych practice.

After all, the right fit is the key to success in any relationship. And for the next fifteen years, I did both therapy and business consulting, and loved every minute of it.

Eventually, in 2006, I decided to make the full-time transition to executive coach, as the 24/7 demands of a therapy practice were just too rigorous for me to endure at that stage of my life. Fortunately, on the forward-looking advice of my mentor a few years earlier, I had already received my PhD in 1998. Finally a doctor, I now had the credentials I needed to tap into the corporate world, even though I recalled hearing so many times growing up that women couldn't be doctors.

The doors were opening wider, right before my eyes.

CHAPTER 5

Common Sense: Don't Leave Home Without It!

You may have heard the idea that people will show up in your life for a reason, a season, or a lifetime. And it can be tough to figure out which timing applies to each of those people.

Fortunately, my first lifelong mentor actually initiated our mentoring relationship, making it easy for me to notice her and to pay attention.

I met Beulah Drom, professor emeritus at the University of Illinois at Urbana-Champaign, when I was a 19-year-old sophomore at the school. She was my professor, and I was terrified of her.

Everybody knew of her no-nonsense reputation as a tough grader. She meant business. And if you weren't serous about your studies, get out of her class.

You see, she was teaching elementary education. And because it's such a big responsibility to teach little children, she wanted to make sure that you were the right person for the job. If you were some flake, or if you weren't serious about your studies, she'd flunk you right out of the class in no time. It was scary. I remember one particular class, when I witnessed someone saying a mean-spirited comment to a child. I said to Professor Drom, "Don't they have any common sense?"

Replying with an observation that I never forgot or took for granted again, Beulah told me, "Common sense is not necessarily common."

About this time, by the second year of my first college career, I had actually been thinking, "you know, maybe school's really not for me." After all, I was the first person in my family to go to college. And after finishing my freshman year, I wasn't convinced yet.

To tell the truth, I was scared that I wasn't good enough, or that I couldn't handle the whole four years.

One day, with approximately seventy-five people in the class, I noticed her handwritten comments in red ink on my paper. I thought,

"Uh-oh, here it is."

But as I turned the paper over in my hands to read it, Beulah's comment made me catch my breath. "Betty, I don't know if you're enjoying being in my class," she had written, "but I'm enjoying having you in mine."

I still have the paper—because with those few words from her red pen, she changed my destiny. My first reaction was amazement. It felt like the big time. I couldn't believe this woman singled me out.

Fortunately, Beulah saw that I had a gift with children, and that I was really good at what I was doing in school. In short, she got it. And Beulah's the first person who made it clear to me!

From that point on, I was drawn to her, and wanted to learn all I could from her. You see, I got it too. I knew that this woman could teach me a lot. I just needed to listen to her, and I needed to trust her.

Beulah Drom, the "teacher's teacher," circa 1955

As it turned out, Beulah advised me for the next thirty-five years.

If I had a problem to figure out, even long after I got out of school, I would call her. And she would give me the most practical advice.

As we discussed each situation, she would say, "Okay, let's look at this now." And then she'd factor in all the things that affected my questions, and eventually, there would be the answer, right in front of us.

Understand, she didn't answer it for me—she'd ask me question after question, leading me to find my own answers.

Essentially, she taught me to ask good questions first.

That's the guided discovery I talk about now and rely on for my own coaching processes to this day. Beulah was the first person that I can recall teaching me that approach. She was so practical and very, very wise.

Beulah didn't have time for games. After all, as the thirteenth child in a farming family that traveled across the country by covered wagon, this woman knew the real value of life and hard work. She was amazing.

Beulah began her journey in life as the thirteenth child of a farming family. They traveled for three months in a covered wagon to journey less than two hundred miles to a Northern Illinois farm, which became their home when Beulah was five years old.

During World War I, Beulah served as a candy striper in a hospital. She was the first person in her family to graduate from both high school and college. She was determined to have a life beyond farming, so Beulah studied nursing and education. During World War II, she was a nurse's aide as well as a schoolteacher.

This woman was so far ahead of her time, and I was fortunate enough to have studied under her and with her. Imagine her journey—from a covered wagon to space shuttles. She really did see it all.

Beulah and I stayed in touch until the day she died. I was even asked to speak at her funeral, because everyone knew how much I loved her, and that she was very special to me.

That's why I went to visit her at least once a year, every year, at the University of Illinois at Champaign, sometimes more often. It was important to me to make a pilgrimage there, spend a day with her, and take her to lunch or dinner.

The best part is, I knew I could trust her implicitly. She wanted nothing from me but for me to be a good person, and to succeed.

Betty O with Professor Beulah Drom

This is the key: I wasn't a threat to her, she wasn't a threat to me, but we both had something to offer. She just wanted me to be good with children, and good at the work I was doing.

Most of all, Beulah taught me that integrity was everything. It wasn't just a word to her, like it is to a lot of people. Many will talk about integrity, but the rest of us don't talk about it because we have it.

In Beulah's words, "Your name, and how you conduct yourself, is everything. They can take everything else away from you, but they can't have that. That's up to you, Betty."

Beulah lived by that principle, and she proved it. In fact, she made big sacrifices during her own career, because she was not political; she didn't necessarily go along with the system.

Unfortunately, she was held back from some opportunities because she wouldn't go along with things that didn't make sense. But she didn't care.

Just the fact that she put that little note on my paper, sparking the connection for both of us, told me that not only did she know what was right, she was proactively going to do her best to prompt it along. And she did.

Her red pen told me she was paying attention to each student, even with so many people in class! Up to that point, I didn't realize she had ever noticed anything that I was doing. Above all, I learned the value of doing what's right in all of your dealings with people.

How do you know what's right? First and foremost, trust your gut. It knows what's right, so listen to what it tells you. Then ask good questions, and don't be afraid of the answers. Better still, put the effort into a little logical analysis. Even better if you do it with a trusted mentor's help, guidance, and perspective.

And finally, use your common sense. Beulah taught me to understand that, if you have common sense, you probably think everyone does. They do not.

Remember, theory and academics will only take you so far. IQ has nothing to do with it either, so developing and using common sense actually gives you a tremendous advantage in business.

Common sense: don't leave home without it!

CHAPTER 6

Without Visibility, You Are Invisible

It's not only important to be good at what you do—that's a given, if you want a successful long-term career.

You also have to be seen—perceived—as an authority, or even the expert, by people on all sides of your circles of influence, including your direct reports, your staff team and supervisors, and your company's upper management chains of command. Plus, it helps to earn recognition from people in your industry, your social circles, and even those you haven't even met yet!

But there's more to it than that. Remember, it's all about your reputation and perception. It's never enough to be brilliant at a particular competency or skill if nobody knows about your expertise.

Even worse, if the way you're perceived creates a reputation that's at odds with the way leaders in your business (or company culture) are generally accepted and looked up to, you're setting yourself up for a steep uphill climb.

I could tell you stories about executives I've coached who had a horrendous conflict between how they thought they were acting and the general perception of their behaviors, and how that discrepancy actually got in the way of their effectiveness or career advancement. In fact, I've mentioned some of them in Chapter 7, "Intent vs. Impact."

But for now, let's look at the best ways to increase your personal and professional visibility for all the right reasons.

Dr. Betty with Eva LaRue, star of CSI Miami

The first year after I launched my psychotherapy practice (much like an executive's first year on the job), I struggled to gain recognition for the value I was bringing to the table.

By this time, my daughter was eight years old. So, with her high school and college years ahead of her, I knew that, eventually, I would be moving to downtown Chicago, in a sink-or-swim effort to expand my business and life prospects in a hurry.

Unfortunately, I was very limited in my circle of friends, which made my professional network very limited too.

Plus, I was single, and I wanted to change my life! So I wasn't going to stay in a community that was all families. I was one of the few divorced people that lived in the community, and I wanted to expand and grow.

Betty O sharing smiles and stories with Carol Channing, Michael Feinstein, and guest

I thought, "Okay, I need to be with different people." That's the lesson—when you want to change your situation, you can't keep doing the same thing!

So, wherever I could, I put myself in different places, and the people I met then opened the door for me to go to my next level. And the next level. And the next. During a particular Kentucky Derby garden party with more than two hundred Chicago socialites, I saw a lot of women who seemed to be brightly dressed, talkative, and even audaciously wealthy. As you can guess, they all played the look-at-me game very well, from the ways they dressed to the cars they drove up in to the ways they talked and the things they talked about.

But from across the yard at one of the track owners' homes, I noticed the most elegant woman I had ever seen. In fact, she stood out from the crowd by virtue of her perfectly sculptured wardrobe and her serene, confident presence.

I knew I had to meet her. But how?

After wringing my hands trying to come up with something clever to say and watching this woman from across the garden for about twenty minutes, I simply walked up to her and said exactly what was on my mind.

"I just had to meet you," I told Bernice as I introduced myself. She was so very gracious and soft-spoken, even in the crowded garden. And as we spoke for those first few minutes, I remember Bernice put out her hand to say she was pleased to meet me, and she held my hand for a long time as we talked.

She looked me directly in the eyes throughout our entire conversation and made me feel like I was the only person present.

With that simple gesture, she taught me 100% attention and focus in the moment. And when Bernice found out I was both a single mother and a successful entrepreneur with four offices in the city, she seemed to be impressed too. We were both being introduced to a lifestyle we had never experienced on our own.

Before the conversation had finished, we agreed to meet for lunch the following day. We instantly hit it off and had so much to talk about!

It turned out that, although Bernice had three sons of her own, she missed the connection that a mother would share with a daughter. And while my own mother was as helpful and giving as she could be, she just didn't know what she didn't know about people, "polite society," and the social graces.

So Bernice and I both had plenty to offer each other as like-minded friends and confidants, and a lifelong mentor relationship was born that day.

After our first encounter more than twenty-five years ago, Bernice took me under her wing and opened my eyes to so many possibilities. She taught me to be involved in many community causes, making certain to give back—and to get some press along the way.

Betty O meeting Bernice Pink for the first time, at a Kentucky Derby party with more than 200 Chicago socialites

Again, that's the thing. You must get your name out there if you want to be successful, both in business and in the corporate world.

Don't worry, being visible doesn't have to mean being outrageous or over the top, though that can work, too, in its place. But to this day, I still remember how Bernice was so quietly elegant, and the most noticeable person at the party.

Besides, meeting new people is fun! It sure was interesting for me. I'm not saying I wanted to be some of the people I met through my expanding network.

But I wanted to learn from them, so I paid attention to their mannerisms and I learned a lot.

One of the most striking advantages my mentors gave me was their insight into more than just what was going on around me at the time. They were able to show me how to predict what was likely to happen tomorrow as a result of today's events, and they guided me to prepare for things I never saw coming.

After creating my brand as an infertility expert with my psych practice, I constantly put the word out to local and national news and popular media when there was nobody else doing what I was from a counseling perspective.

Fortunately, my specialty had come about from my own genuine interest and need, as my former husband and I had struggled to have kids when we were married. After researching, writing, and publishing a book on the subject, my infertility counseling was the first service of its kind worldwide, and became my unique brand almost immediately.

But I knew I had to move quickly, as others would follow suit within the next year or so (nothing stays unique for long). After all, if people read about you, hear about you on radio and see you on television, you must be the expert. And I had plenty to say about my specialty to the various newspapers, magazines, and television reporters I developed relationships with.

Within a few years, with the observations and predictions of Bernice and several of my other mentors to guide me, I started to see the writing on the wall. Long before today's planned-care restrictions and regulations, insurance companies were starting to set limits on the number of cases any given practice was eligible to handle.

That's why I agreed to take on business clients through my friend's counseling firm, supplementing my income opportunities, my experience, and my network at the same time. Once again, my mentors' foresight ended up shaping my career in a way I hadn't even imagined a few short years earlier.

I know that, because of Bernice's mentorship, I've met people with influence, connections, and power, and developed a tremendous network. Right about now, you might be thinking, "What does that have to do with my career or my job as an executive?"

Well, remember, it is a small world. What you know, and more importantly who you know, can make all of the difference to your career. Your visibility–being seen or being included at functions with industry experts, business celebrities and other notables–adds to your credibility.

After all, winners associate with winners, don't they? At least, that is the common operating assumption.

Plus, there are added bonuses that come your way as a result of these associations–better tables at restaurants, a phone call that is returned rather than ignored, or an invitation that might generate another opportunity, more connections, or more business for your company.

At the very least, you might find yourself at a fabulous dinner or party. Over the years, through Bernice's generosity as my mentor, I was introduced to Hollywood royalty, and frequently attend amazing social gatherings to this day.

Betty O with Bernice Pink, 25 years later

VISIBILITY LEADS TO OPPORTUNITIES

Keep in mind, you never know where you might get another referral.

I was attending a wake of a prominent physician's father-in-law. I did not know the deceased, but out of respect to the physician who had always been gracious to me (as well as a mentor), I attended the wake.

As I was about to leave, a gentleman approached me and asked how I knew the deceased. It turns out he was the brother of my physician and mentor, and we had a lovely conversation.

After I discovered he was a very prominent divorce attorney, this man asked me what I did for my career.

I told him I was a psychotherapist, and that I shared office space with his brother.

His eyes widened. Coincidentally, he had a client in need of therapy for herself and her children, so we exchanged contact details, even though I had never considered the possibility of getting clients at a wake!

This is a great example of the halo effect. In that attorney's mind, I must have been good at what I do, too–considering his brother was sharing his office space with me and putting my name on the door.

Fortunately, he was right, and this attorney became a steady source of referrals for many years to come.

Who you are matters. Who and what you are associated with matters. What you are known for matters. It's not who you know that matters nearly as much as who knows you.

So get visible for the right things–the ones that enhance your reputation, bring you close to your goals, and further your career. Get visible for the person you are, not the things you own.

But above all, get visible!

LIES YOU'VE BEEN TOLD; THE TRUTH WILL SET YOU FREE

Three lies you've been told:

1. Your GPA (grade point average) is crucial.
2. Your college degree is a guarantee.
3. Your hard work will assure your success.

These lies may not even get you an interview, let alone a job or career. Sorry, but times are different today. You are now competing globally for just about everything. And the corporate world isn't a glee club.

THREE TRUTHS TO LIVE BY

1. Nobody does it alone; mentors and coaches are absolutely necessary for high-level success.
2. You win when you distinguish yourself from others and create your brand. You need to stand out (for the right reasons, of course).
3. Developing excellent people skills is a double-win, for you and your network.

Of course, there are many other lies and truths you'll hear in business, but these three are not negotiable if you desire sustainable success in the corporate world.

What separates the 1% from the rest of us? It's not just luck or being born under the right star. It's actually having the right person in your corner.

As a master performance coach, I help people just like you who want to rise through the ranks and grab that brass ring. I've learned the true value of investing in yourself as the foundation of a fulfilling career and life. Remember, nobody does it alone!

CHAPTER 7

Intent vs. Impact

I am often surprised by the impact of one's style and words. I know that, in the thirty-plus years I have been coaching, I have seen many people unintentionally destroy morale and embarrass, humiliate, and hurt other people.

Did they get up in the morning and say to themselves, "I am going to be a jerk today and create chaos and pain"? No, that is not their intent, but that's still their impact on others.

When I coach someone, I always reserve a day very early on in the process to shadow and observe them in action. It gives me a firsthand view of their style of communication, how they relate to people, whether they ask or tell, etc.

It also creates a wonderful opportunity to really see for myself what the dynamics are with their team. I notice how others view them and what their relationships are to one another. Shadowing provides a real jump-start to the coaching process.

On one occasion, a Fortune 100 company that I did a lot coaching for engaged me to do post-hire coaching for one of their officers.

She had just come into the company, and unfortunately, there were already some problems starting to show up. People on her team were not performing up to their usual standards—not even close!

Within the first few minutes of my shadowing sessions with her, I saw what the problems were. From where I sat, it was obvious.

And to set the stage, you have to know she had a brilliant, brilliant mind. She had graduated from an Ivy League school and had a reputation for intelligence. She also knew the deliverables of her job very well. This woman was committed to excellence and had an outstanding work ethic.

In fact, she genuinely cared about her team, but her style said something quite different. The trouble was, she had no clue about her impact on her team—none.

When it came to communicating with her staff, it seemed that she did everything wrong. I think if there were ten things that you shouldn't do, she did them all. She did eleven!

I knew that this would be one of my more challenging assignments, as this woman was truly blind to how she talked to people. Unfortunately, while I knew she cared about the people on her team and the impact she could have on them, she cared more about her own ego and about getting her own way.

Keep in mind, she was an officer of a major company, so this was a big job. You need to have a solid ego to hold a position like that. But this was at a whole other level.

Even though she delivered them in the worst possible way, her comments were usually accurate. She honestly believed that if she was stating a fact, there shouldn't be a problem.

As you can imagine, nobody wanted to work for her. In fact, they avoided her whenever possible, which certainly doesn't make for a great functioning team. As smart as she was, she couldn't see what was happening on her own.

As part of a 360-degree interview, I conducted twenty face-to-face interviews with her team, her peers, and her superiors in order to get the actual context of each individual's confidential comments. Then I sanitized the answers to further protect people's identities.

As she read my report afterwards, the executive I was coaching admitted that this was not the first time she had experienced these problems. Nor was this the first time she had been told about the reasons why. But it just wasn't getting through.

In the end, I did not continue coaching her, as she was not engaged, and it seemed her ego was doing all of the talking. My recommendation to the company was to not invest in coaching if the subject is not on board. She was offered a very lucrative severance package and moved on.

You can be sure we carefully interviewed new candidates to assure the proper fit, for both their competencies and the corporate culture. After all, you can be the best coach in the world, but you must know your limitations and accept if someone isn't interested. You get much better results by coaching someone who is!

The IQ was there, but the EQ was not.

CHAPTER 8

The Key to Connecting

Here's a fun example that demonstrates the awesome power of connecting in order to build that relationship with your clients or team members as people.

One day, I received a phone call from a CEO who had a scheduled meeting with me for 1:00 p.m. on that same day. I was going to be presenting a formal proposal to him, and I had not actually met him in person previously.

On the call, he asked me if there was any way I could move the appointment to an earlier time; otherwise, he would have to reschedule for another day. I said sure, I would be there within the hour.

Trouble was, I was not in my business clothes at that moment. I was at my office in downtown Chicago and did not have time to go home and change into a business suit.

However, I arrived at corporate headquarters on schedule and the CEO greeted me warmly and thanked me for the accommodation. He saw I was carrying what appeared to be a gym bag and he graciously took it out of my hands to carry it for me.

When he then commented on how heavy the bag was, the bag wiggled vigorously. So, as we sat down, I explained that my Jack Russell terrier, Madison, was with me for the morning, and in order to accommodate the change in our meeting time, I came directly to his office.

Right there at his desk, we unzipped the bag and Madison sat on this man's lap for the entire presentation. Within minutes, the CEO connected with me on our mutual love for dogs. He saw the warm side of me, and we were in sync as people before beginning the business part of the meeting.

By that time, he already liked me, he was already in a good mood, and I had his attention. He let down his guard because my dog was so charming.

When we started to talk financials, he told me my services were three times the price of the other two coaches.

I replied that it was a customized program and would be worth every penny. He said he was inclined to believe me—besides, he loved my dog!

Yes, Madison closed the deal. And the situation reminded me to never underestimate the power of connecting, establishing relationships, and building rapport.

There really is no substitute for good relationships as the foundation for good business!

Here's a revealing exercise I do with my clients all the time.

Ask yourself which of your teachers you remember from school.

That question usually gets people thinking. They remember the bad ones and they remember the good ones.

What's really revealing is they don't usually remember what the content was with either teacher. I know that, even with my own favorite teachers, I don't remember details of the subjects they taught me.

All I remember is how they made me feel.

So if somebody made you feel great, or smart, you remember them. You also remember the ones who made you feel stupid or who embarrassed you.

Even all these years later, how those teachers made people feel is what students will remember. We remember the names of those people who made a strong impression on us; all those other teachers fall by the wayside–they don't touch us somehow.

Understand the power of that and you won't ever leave anybody hanging with a negative impression you don't want. Be aware of what people are feeling when you are speaking. Because if you make the wrong kind of connection with somebody early on, they will remember that forever too. Fail to make a connection, and you will be invisible and dismissed.

CHAPTER 9

The Power of Listening

Though it may seem counterintuitive, the best way to be heard is to listen first. You've already read about the regional vice president of a very prominent corporation who was very accomplished but often at the expense of others. Her standards were very high, but that was not the problem.

The problem was her style of communication. She didn't listen to her staff, so they didn't feel heard, didn't make a connection with her, and didn't feel motivated to perform well.

KNOW YOURSELF FIRST. ARE YOUR BLIND SPOTS OPPORTUNITIES OR BARRIERS?

Here's a story of another client experience (one that turned out to be a huge victory for the executive, his team, the corporation, and the executive's family). It demonstrates a related and valuable lesson here too.

Sitting in on several live meetings with this executive, it quickly became very obvious to me that the problem was his way of talking down to people, interrupting them when they spoke, and always leaving them with a negative feeling.

Was this his intent? Absolutely not. He genuinely cared about the people on his team and would always compensate and reward them financially. However, emotionally they were left bruised and confused.

As I began to coach him, it became apparent he was not really making the connection that his style of communication was the reason for his team not wanting to participate in meetings. Everyone was afraid to be embarrassed and criticized publicly. Can you blame them?

Taking a more hands-on approach, I decided to act exactly like him during a few of our coaching sessions. I would bait him by asking him questions, then interrupt his reply almost immediately. As we continued our coaching session in this way, I could see how frustrated and how visibly upset he was becoming. But I persisted for a few more minutes, stopping just short of making him leap across the table to choke me!

I then asked him how it felt. How did it feel to be interrupted, not to be listened to, and to have someone talking over him? I explained that his approach was doing exactly that to others. To my surprise, there were now tears streaming down his face. He got it.

The good news is that this man became aware of his blind spots and took the necessary steps to correct them. We developed a script for him to practice until it became natural to him to include the new words in his responses.

Did it pay off for him? From time to time, I still hear from this executive and his wife, and his career and their family's happiness quotient are both scoring high. You see, he's learned to listen and communicate better at home as well.

So yes, it was worth it.

EMAIL IS YOUR FRIEND, EXCEPT WHEN IT ISN'T

Because I pride myself on serving my clients and not just advising, I am very responsive to emails, I return calls, and I am respectful of my clients' time. One very late evening (actually well into the wee hours of the morning), I heard my computer ding, signaling I had just received an email.

This was a request from the president of a Fortune 500 company I was working with, but where I had not met the president as yet. So I quickly responded to her message, hoping to impress her.

Especially since it was 2:00 a.m., I thought I would demonstrate that they could count on me any time of day. Confidently pressing the Send button, I did not proofread the email; after all, I knew what I had said.

The next day, I received a call from the head of HR of this firm. Apparently, I had my fingers on the wrong keys and sent a completely garbled message. Not only was I embarrassed, but this executive was very unforgiving, and I never did business with that firm again. It was a very costly and embarrassing mistake.

I had one other mishap prior to this one, when I was writing a funny note to one of my closest friends. It was naughty and filled with fun. But as soon as I hit Send, I realized it went to the president of the European division of a Fortune 500 company, not my buddy Tony. I was mortified.

A short time later, I received a message from Tony, the president, saying, though this was not intended for him, thanks for making him laugh so hard. Fortunately, this man had a great sense of humor and was delightful. In fact, he loved my sense of humor so much, we connected and continue to have a business relationship today.

That was fifteen years ago. I just plain got lucky that time. But you can be sure I triple check all correspondence going out these days. I suggest you do as well.

WHO ARE YOU WHEN NOBODY'S WATCHING?

I like to assess people casually, in informal situations when they're not mindful of being on their best behavior. That is when you really see who they are. Are they rude to the waitress? Do they pass the security guard without a greeting? Are they dismissive to subordinates?

What you see is really what you get when people are just doing their thing. Kind, respectful people are just that across the board, not just to their boss, their clergy, or people of influence.

You know what I've noticed? Raised voices are not necessary. Demeaning behavior is always unacceptable. We are all women, men, moms, dads, sisters, brothers, sons, daughters, and friends—and we all deserve respect, courtesy, and kindness.

These things are free, and they are choices we make. Only we can decide what kind of human being we choose to be. These things are not DNA-determined, but rather a choice that we can all decide to make for ourselves. And don't kid yourself, the consequences of those choices are very real too.

In other words, what you choose now will have definite consequences, now and later. The consequences can and will be very positive if you make great decisions. Life will also be less stressful and more pleasurable if you choose to be respectful and kind.

After all, people go out of their way for kindness, and human nature proves time and time again that virtually everyone gets even with nasty people by losing the report, not providing a timely return call, or holding up the flow of progress with many other passive aggressive actions.

Remember, people are always assessing you too, either informally or formally. Just because you don't hear about it doesn't mean people aren't talking about you and forming opinions.

The administrative assistants in your organization all talk to one another and know the office tea. Trust me, if you are a cocky jerk who is rude and demanding, it might take a long time to get that appointment on the calendar.

On the other hand, if you are thoughtful, pleasant, and have a sense of humor, they will tend to get you on the calendar quickly–even if they have to switch someone else out.

There are actually so many positives to being a nice person, I don't understand why everyone doesn't act that way by default. Isn't it common sense?

Oh, wait a minute, I forgot that common sense is not necessarily common. As I've said before–but it's worth repeating–common sense can take you farther than the highest IQ. Never underestimate the power of common sense.

EVER MET YOUR WORST ENEMY FACE-TO-FACE?

Over the course of the years, I have worked with so many talented people, it never ceases to amaze me how people are often their own worst enemy. Sure, capitalize on your strengths, but there's no need for overkill.

I was working with an extremely talented young man who was about to be promoted yet again. For this project, the organization had engaged me to onboard this executive into a new role. He had risen rapidly over the years and had established himself as someone who was on the "fast track."

Naturally, the organization wanted to ensure his success, as the first ninety days in any new position or company are critical in determining the perception people will develop about you. How we present ourselves, and whether we engage others or not, are impressions people walk away with—and they have a surprisingly long shelf life. Coming in as a maverick is rarely a good strategy inside corporate walls.

The thing is, this young man was truly amazing, and he knew it. So I coached him on being careful to let his new team and division discover this for themselves. I advised him that, even if he was certain he had the answer, it would be best to ask his team what was working, what they would like to see happening in the next few quarters, and how they could get there.

Letting his team know that what they thought and wanted actually mattered to him was not only my suggested introductory strategy for him, but an enormously valuable ongoing strategy to adopt. He'd get much better buy-in from his team members if they knew that he was indeed an inclusive leader who would value their ideas.

Besides, I knew that his reputation was one of getting things done at any cost. He valued results over people and for the long term he would not be successful if he continued on this path.

WHEN YOUR EGO DOES THE TALKING

We rehearsed scenarios and prepped for his first meeting with his team, a group of very talented and experienced people. Most of them were fifteen to twenty years older than this young executive. This was going to be a delicate introduction, as I wanted him to start off by making them feel valued and letting them know how lucky he was to have their experience and expertise on his side.

What's that saying about "the best-laid plans"?

Walking into his first team meeting without even a greeting, the young executive proceeded to inform everyone there would be many changes. He told the group that he couldn't believe they were still doing things the way they were, and that they were behind the times.

Suffice it to say, his introduction was a disaster (Hint: never trash the past). But from there, he went on to tell everyone about all of his victories and how smart he was. You can imagine how he was received!

In short, he may have had all of the talent in the world, but his ego went unchecked. At least he demonstrated a perfect example of what not to do.

I ultimately decided it would be better to work with his team to help them adapt and adjust to him, rather than coaching this young man. You see, even though he urgently needed to change his behavior to change his team's results, he clearly did not think that he needed coaching, nor did he want it.

Lesson learned? Again, talent alone is not enough. For best results, be sure to check your ego at the door– or better yet, leave it at home!

Check the following list of behaviors that can make or break your career. Are you including all the must-dos in and eliminating all the don't-dares from your workplace conduct?

MUST-DOS & DON'T-DARES

Must Do
- Speaking up and saying you will do something

Don't Dare
- Forgetting about doing it, or not following through

Must Do
- Committing to do something on time

Don't Dare
- Missing the due date, without letting people in charge know about the change

---

Must Do
- Taking on responsibilities that help the organization further its goals along with your own

Don't Dare
- Not letting others know when there is a problem or when you need help, causing embarrassment or a crisis for everyone involved

---

Must Do
- Getting to the root cause of performance issues

Don't Dare
- Blaming others (teammates, other departments, the boss) when things go wrong

---

Must Do
- Presenting a potential solution with every problem you bring to your superior's attention

Don't Dare
- Voicing complaints (repeatedly), without offering solutions or participating in finding them

Must Do
- Meeting new challenges with enthusiasm and an open mind

Don't Dare
- Always being the naysayer when changes are discussed and resisting anything new

....

Must Do
- Recognizing your team for their accomplishments

Don't Dare
- Focusing on your personal success at the expense or exclusion of others

....

Must Do
- Always striving to give your best effort

Don't Dare
- Settling for mediocrity in your performance

....

Must Do
- Admitting your mistakes and finding ways to correct them

Don't Dare
- Failing to apologize or take ownership when you make a mistake, and thus not learning from it either

....

Must Do
- Earning your place by working to help your organization succeed

Don't Dare
- Expecting to be rewarded or promoted just for showing up to work, without demonstrating high performance (thinking you are entitled)

Negative behaviors create mistrust. In other words, if you persist in repeating the "don't-dare" actions listed above, no one can depend on you. You have made yourself useless. No one can feel safe with you and you have become a liability. You certainly won't be contributing to achieving successful results or an effective and safe organization with that in your bio!

CHAPTER 10

Crying at Work: There Will Be Consequences

Have you ever wanted to cry at work?

Of course, many times you will be disappointed, upset, frustrated, or so mad you could spit. But let me give you a piece of career-saving advice: you must not cry.

As Tom Hanks's character says in the movie *A League of Their Own,* "There's no crying in baseball!" Well, there's no crying in business either. Unless you are looking for pity; then go for it. However, pity will not get you to the corner office or the C-suite.

Crying at work is seen as the sign of a weak or excessively emotional person. This may not actually be true, but it is often interpreted that way. Remember, as women, we have enough biases to contend with. Don't add crying to your list.

In the past thirty years, I have witnessed crying as a career killer.

A few years ago, I worked with a woman who was incredibly talented. She's a great executive and one of the smartest people I know. But she was also a very sensitive person. And the business world can be a tough place for women.

After all, you know, guys get tough. She would get emotional during a meeting or a heated discussion. Unfortunately, she would also get her feelings hurt because she'd take things personally.

And she'd cry—tears would come down her face in the moment.

The thing is, guys don't like that. Actually, nobody likes that, because crying makes people uncomfortable. They don't know how to respond to it, so they want to get rid of it.

After all, most men are used to fixing things. The truth is, we're not asking them to fix anything. But that's how they take it when they see someone cry and it makes them uneasy.

Women cry, and when we cry with each other, it's fine, as an emotional release or even just as another way of communicating.

Women don't usually judge it. Men—it makes them so uncomfortable because they don't know how to fix it.

Returning to my executive client, eventually nobody wanted to work with her. And when this went on for a few years, they used it against her. It ruined her reputation.

THE KISS OF DEATH

The trouble is, as women, we already have a strike against us in the corporate world—like it or not, it's not necessarily an advantage to be a woman in business today. They will use whatever they can find to nail you with.

My client eventually had to leave that company because she wasn't going to go any further. It was both infuriating and expensive, since this woman was ten times more talented than the guys she was working with!

She could have been the CEO of the company. But because she was sensitive by nature and would cry when upset, she was prevented from meeting her potential.

It was the kiss of death to her career path.

I mean, if somebody died, that would be one thing. But the guys were threatened by her because she was smarter, ten times quicker, and more knowledgeable than they were. They were looking for a reason to dismiss her.

So they held her emotions against her. And it was an easy weapon to wield.

After she got out of that company, she learned how to manage her emotions and walk away from situations that presented difficulty.

In time, she became very successful at a big job with another company. But it was painful, a hard lesson for her. Besides, the damage that was done at the first company was inescapable as long as she was there. And it was all so unnecessary!

After all, it's very hurtful to know you're right about something and they aren't going to listen because of their preconceptions, earned or otherwise. People will tend to discount you before you ever come in.

So if you need to cry, leave the office. Excuse yourself from a meeting. Do whatever you have to do in order to preserve your image.

Again, she was as sharp a woman as I have ever met. But it took years of getting out of that business and getting into another business before she learned to lock it up and wait until she got home, or whatever she had to do.

Even though it's not recommended either, an angry outburst would have been better than one tear. If she had turned around and pushed right back, they'd have respected her.

But when they saw a tear, they knew they had her. She lost their respect and they had a weapon.

When I realized what was happening with her, we made addressing the problem a cornerstone of her coaching sessions for weeks. She learned to separate her feelings out, to not take things so personally, and to walk it off–to leave the room to excuse herself and regroup.

You do whatever it takes. When you feel the emotions starting to rise past your breaking point, say "I've got a phone call," or simply "Excuse me," or whatever it takes in the situation.

Actually, that goes for both women and men. I have guys who had trouble controlling their emotions as well. It doesn't matter whether it's tears or reaching a point where they're ready to blow and tell off their boss. They can't do it. They're going to get fired if they do.

Instead, I get them to excuse themselves and leave the room. Because you can't cry, or explode, in front of your colleagues, your superiors, or your team. That's why you have to learn to exit the situation while your composure is still intact.

I had a guy that I worked with at the New York Stock Exchange. He cried during a particularly stressful trading day, and his career was over.

Because they all made fun of him. His career was toast.

Remember, these were advanced and strategic competitors, big players. They will look for one weakness and they'll go for the kill.

The moral of the story is don't let your weaknesses show. We all have them. But don't let them show!

Maybe that's why I'm not in the corporate world as an employee anymore. I'm sure that many times, I would be crying too, I'd be so pissed off!

You must remember, though, that you can handle anything that comes up because you still have the control, and you have the independence to separate your personal self-worth from events happening around you.

That's how to think about your vulnerabilities. Everybody's got some. But if you show them, they will be used against you.

Also, don't whine about what is not fair or what someone said or did. Suck it up. The world is not fair, and you are going to be tested. Nobody wants to hear someone complain. It is draining and negative.

Look at Danica Patrick, the race driver—she's a crybaby! Watching her complain and tear down her crew, her car, and her competitors after a race was excruciating.

Think about it. When you're competing in a man's game like racing, you don't come off the track and say, "He bumped me," and cry about it.

I wanted to say, "Honey, that's what you do in racing so use your talents to play the game you're in!"

I wish I'd been her coach, because she'd be a winner. She was talented enough, but she kept playing the girlie-girl card. And boy, she already had the deck stacked against her in that industry, but then being a crybaby too?

By the way, you're miles ahead when you get a coach or a therapist. Because even your family doesn't want to hear your complaints. And to be fair, they may not know how to deal with the demands of your industry or profession either.

KEEP YOUR COMPOSURE AT WORK

Above all, don't take things personally at work. If you do, you will frequently be found crying, defending yourself, or doing some other behavior that will be labeled unprofessional. The key is to remove yourself until you can regroup emotionally.

Think about a tug of war with a rope. When one person lets go, there is no war. Of course, the best advice is to avoid getting involved from the start. But if you inadvertently find yourself participating in a power struggle, remove yourself as quickly as possible. In other words, drop the rope.

Remember, power struggles draw attention for the wrong reasons. Simply remove yourself gracefully—and immediately.

Being involved in a power struggle is, at best, a waste of time. At worst, it can ruin a reputation because the players are guilty by association. As my good friend Ema Savahl (fashion designer to the stars) once told me, "Your reputation is more important than your eyes."

I think that pretty much says it all. I mean, to me, your eyes are the most important of all the senses. So don't let someone else's behavior savage your reputation. Don't sacrifice your reputation for something that you can just as easily overlook, ignore, or walk away from.

After all, you will witness many power struggles throughout your personal and professional lifetimes.

When the egos go at it, somebody will lose. Don't let it be you. You will be judged by your decisions, your actions, and your associations. Be cognizant of this at all times.

When in doubt, take the time to consider the possible outcomes, how people will be impacted, and the timing of your decisions. Then choose wisely based on the information you have at hand at the moment.

For example, the wrong action at the right time is a mistake. But the right action at the wrong time will also result in resistance.

You want to have a reputation that demonstrates good business acumen and well-thought-out decisions. You are building your reputation every day. And power struggles are about ego, not about solving a problem.

There will be people that will make you want to scream. Don't engage. If you do, they will win. Whether they have anxiety disorder or are lonely, it really doesn't matter. How you manage the situation is key.

Generally, these people have boundary issues, so keep your door closed. Not that a closed door will stop them, but at least it will demonstrate to you how rude they really are.

Their motivation doesn't matter either. Forget about trying to understand why or trying to fix them. All you can do is to manage the situation.

For example, I had one executive that would "hold everyone hostage" on his team, especially when people were trying to get to their trains home at the end of the day.

My guess is that he was really very lonely. But he would call subordinates into his office, usually one at a time, and as they would try to exit, he would walk over and block the door. Or he'd put his hand on their shoulder to make a point or think of "just one more thing" that had to be discussed.

Observing his staff at work, I noticed that when his name was mentioned, people were immediately and visibly stressed. If they saw him walking toward them, they would quickly duck into someone else's office.

The best we can do with a situation like this is to take charge. Remind this individual a few minutes before the end of the meeting that you will be leaving or that you have another meeting to attend. If they keep talking, politely tell them that you will get back to them or email them with another time, etc.

Plus, do not feel guilty when you leave. People like this play on their coworkers being polite and not wanting to hurt others' feelings. They have no consideration for anyone but themselves. They derive pleasure from controlling others because it feels very powerful to them.

Simply take your power back and carry yourself with confidence and grace (nobody wants to follow a wimp). If necessary, stand near the door or arrange for your administrative assistant to come and get you at a designated time. Your time is valuable, and you needn't be held hostage anymore.

Whenever possible, meet such a person in a public place or your own office, to minimize their control. You can even secretly find ways to amuse yourself by predicting what they will say or do and being prepared for their tactics.

Either way, take control—or they will control you.

And above all, do not let your vulnerabilities show. People will be happy to take the opportunity to exploit them—and believe me, other women will use them too! It's not just a man thing.

If you're smarter, better, more successful, or a threat to someone else's position, people are looking for your vulnerabilities. And it's certainly true in Hollywood, in politics, in corporate life, anywhere. It's human nature.

So don't worry. When they look at you and say to themselves, "Okay, what's your weakness?" you're going to have some. You just don't need to let everybody know what they are!

By the way, when a challenging situation comes up that you need help dealing with or figuring out, talk it through with somebody else who doesn't work at the company. Because if you're thinking of trusting your colleagues or other team members with your vulnerabilities and the future of your career, my advice is don't do it.

Even if they don't hurt you with it today, they may do so later. Or they may accidentally let something slip and not mean it in a bad way. But then somebody else can grab it and run with it, leaving your career in the dust.

The business world is not an imaginary garden or some other pretty place. Protect yourself.

CHAPTER 11

The Five Habits
Holding Women Back

As a lifelong learner, I know the value of listening, reading and observing. I do it automatically—whether I am in a store, an airport, or a restaurant, I find myself studying people. I enjoy doing it and often make it into a game. I also fully believe we must share what we learn with others. In doing so we help others, and they in turn will be more open to sharing with us, if not today, then perhaps some time in the future. Sharing generates goodwill, shows we care, and could lead to an opportunity that would otherwise have been missed.

I read two to three books per week. They are all of value, even the ones I think miss the boat. We learn from every situation if we pay attention. Yes, I go to school on everyone. I want to share a great read with you.

Sally Helgesen is a leadership expert. Her book *How Women Rise* is excellent and I highly recommend you read it. I suggest you not only familiarize yourself with the twelve bad habits in her book, but that you memorize them to make certain you are on your best game. Winners take action!

The habits Helgesen warns against are all ones that uniquely plague women. Whether from cultural upbringing or intrinsic female qualities, women often simply have a different way of approaching problems, interpersonal relationships, and their own long-term career goals. In order to succeed in the business world, we need to level the playing field by being aware of these pitfalls and consciously avoiding them.

As girls, many of us were taught that being "good" meant keeping quiet, having good manners, and being agreeable. As a result, women are notoriously wary of touting their own accomplishments. Instead, they wait patiently for recognition, without realizing that they need to speak up and be their own best salesperson. If you don't advocate for yourself, you will end up resentful and disappointed. First put in the work to gain competency, then make sure your superiors know about it!

Another stereotypical female trait is letting our feelings get in the way of getting ahead. We genuinely care what others think of us, and don't want to be seen as aggressive, rude, or eager to take advantage of others. The problem is, men don't have the same qualms that women do. They were encouraged from a young age to go after their goals without taking into consideration how others felt about their actions.

You need to do the same! There's no need to be rude about it, but putting your own needs first, seeking out people who will help you reach your goals, and then using their support to lift yourself up–these are not things to be ashamed of. They are essential business tactics you will need to learn to utilize as well as your male counterparts do, if you want your success to rival theirs.

I encourage you to pick up Helgesen's book to learn more about the traps that women fall into, and how to avoid them. Once again, I remind the reader to share what you have learned. Pass these tips on to others. You will be helping others, and that is a reward in and of itself. Pay it forward now!

In my years of experience as both a professional coach and as a woman, I have identified and observed five habits that are unique to women and have proven to be problematic. Nobody wins with the following habits:

1. Dwelling on the past
2. Perfectionism
3. Being overly amenable
4. Giving away your credit
5. Waiting for recognition

Dwelling on the past is a habit unique to women. A woman will have a conversation with a colleague, then second-guess if she chose the right words or right timing and how she left the other person feeling. Men have the same conversation and move right along. They do not ask themselves if they said too much, hurt the other person's feelings, or spoke at the wrong time. They just move on. Dwelling is unproductive and diminishes the ability to be effective. It is a waste of time and energy!

Perfectionism is a set up for disappointment, and it is stressful. Perfection is not possible. Make your goal good enough, then move on!

You can't please everyone. So often women try to do it all. You must delegate and be assertive. Too much time and energy is spent on making nice. Make a decision and take action, period.

Don't give your credit away, even by failing to speak up and take it. Our work does not necessarily speak for itself. Men don't hesitate to credit themselves. Be ready to blow your own horn or someone else will be taking the credit!

Don't wait for recognition for your work. Advocate for yourself or you will end up resentful and disappointed!

These habits are truly foes for women. In order to succeed women must be aware of how they operate and what habits or behaviors are useful and which are destructive. These habits clearly keep women stuck and must be kept in check!

CHAPTER 12

Trust and Kindness: The Secret Sauce

Over the course of my career, I have worked with several individuals who were brilliant, talented visionaries–people who were committed to the bottom line and had exceptional communication skills.

Seems like the perfect combination, right?

Well, almost. The problem was, they could not be trusted, which will kill any career long term.

If you are a leader, it's important to say what you mean, and mean what you say. Your team must know that you have their backs and that you are providing direction with integrity and good ethics. Without these attributes, you will demoralize your staff, get dragged down with turnover issues, and may even face potential legal issues.

It has been my experience that these non-trustworthy individuals' egos are overinflated. They honestly believe that they are smarter than the people around them, and that they can persuade and charm their way through the world at large.

One individual comes to mind who had all the "right stuff" on paper–experience, education, a well-spoken demeanor, tremendous work ethic, intelligence, excellent verbal and written communication skills, and professional appearance.

But something was missing. As it turned out, nobody trusted him because he was a "sniper." He had the need to eliminate all competition, real or imagined, at any cost. The truth is, he had the talent to be a CEO of a Fortune 500 company. So it was a shame to watch this executive sabotage his own career with his gaming behavior.

Unfortunately, the impact of his behavior affected not just his own success but the careers of many other talented executives who exited the organization as a result of working with this man. The lost opportunity cost for the organization could not be measured.

Not surprisingly, everyone was aware of the problems he created, but nobody confronted him because his numbers were always good. Imagine what his numbers could have been if he had rallied and inspired others working for and with him!

This was a huge missed opportunity and short-sighted on the organization's part–a problem that's not so uncommon.

KINDNESS IS KEY

Like you, sometimes I love watching celebrities and their glamorous lifestyles. The parties, the limos, their huge mansions and huge personalities . . . it's like a quick trip to fantasyland, where you can almost live vicariously through their celebrated, charmed lives.

In the late 1980s, I was at the International Film Festival in Chicago with my date, a photographer who was shooting photos of the crowd for the event.

Suddenly, in walked this glamorous red-haired woman who seemed to part the crowd around her. She appeared to be about seventy years of age and looked just like Arlene Dahl–stunning!

I didn't recognize her, but I figured she was a movie star. She had a cigarette holder about as long as her arm, and as she placed a cigarette between her lips to light it, I grabbed the lighter out of some guy's hand, walked right over, and lit her cigarette for her.

I didn't know what made me do it, but I needed to meet her. She just looked at me and said "Oh, thank you, love," with her British accent. "You have kind eyes." We started talking and she said, "What a dear girl you are; let's have lunch together."

Naturally, she let me buy the lunch (which I could barely afford), but Sascha soon became my second mentor, in ways I'd never expected.

Mentors Irene Alexander (concert pianist), Mamie Walton (socialite), and grand dame Sascha

During the next few years and as often as I wanted to accompany her, Sascha took me to a lot of parties, galas, and grand openings with a whole new crowd of people to meet. Of course, she wanted me to drive, but it didn't matter why, because in taking me to these parties, she taught me to get involved with charity work too.

She would have me pick her up and we would trade stories as I escorted her to these fabulous parties.

For example, as we got to know each other better, I discovered that Sascha had been one of the ladies on Jackie Kennedy's historic White House restoration committee during the early sixties. Jackie and Sascha became good friends for years after that.

And as I mentioned, Sascha was a beauty too, so when she told me how JFK would "look you up and down and undress you with his eyes," I was both horrified and fascinated. I started to realize that, although I didn't want to be like them, I could learn a lot from watching this new crowd.

You see, as glamorous as she was, Sascha was just a person like you and me, with her own blend of fixations and foibles to go along with the glitter. I learned both good and bad things from her. And it wasn't long before I realized that, although she loved me like a daughter, she would turn on anybody.

For example, when I met Sascha, she was married to the billionaire who owned the largest trading company in the world. He was one of the richest men in the world at the time too, so needless to say, they had a few bucks.

As it turned out, both of them were absolutely fixated on money, to the point that Sascha would steal the tips off the table when we'd go to a restaurant!

I'd get so embarrassed, I would run back in to put down another tip, because she was so awful about money. Or she'd eat three-quarters of the meal and send it back and say "That was terrible! That was rotten!" I mean, this money thing was a sickness with her.

I'll never forget that. But at the same time, I have to give Sascha credit for changing my life in countless ways, especially through the people I met as a result of our friendship with her as my mentor.

DON'T UNDERESTIMATE THE POWER OF KINDNESS

One day while I waited in the lobby to take Sascha to a doctor's appointment (she was in her late seventies then, and I was forty-five), a man started coughing and wheezing near me. I thought he was the custodian, as he had a baseball cap on and was dressed casually (this was a very upscale building).

I approached him, asked if he was OK, and offered to get him a drink of water. His reply was, "No, but thank you, young lady. That is very kind of you." He introduced himself to me as Senator Bernard Neistein. Then he asked me to come back and visit with him (he was ninety-two at the time).

What a wonderful relationship and mentorship this evolved into as the result of a simple act of kindness!

Long story short, the senator helped my daughter by providing a reference for her academic scholarship to Boston College and made countless invaluable introductions. He owned banks and helped me get a mortgage with one phone call. He also taught me about politics and negotiations. I miss him dearly, especially his stories about the Mafia during the Kennedy election.

The senator was my first male mentor. We need mentors of all ages, backgrounds, and genders. Don't limit yourself, as each one has gifts and wisdom to offer. You can learn from everyone.

Be kind to everyone; everyone deserves respect. The bonus of little acts of kindness is that they feel good to do, and you meet some darn nice people! **Kindness is key and it is free!**

CHAPTER 13

Branding and Blind Spots

Your reputation follows you everywhere. And it doesn't just follow you from behind; it actually precedes you and arrives in the room for a meeting long before you do.

So do yourself a favor. Make sure you create a brand for yourself that serves you well and with distinction, both with people you've met and the others who have yet to be so lucky!

Your brand can mean two different things to people:

· What you are known **for**
· What you are known **as**

In actual fact, your brand includes both of those elements. In other words, you may be known for your brilliant organizational mind or your creative promotional solutions to any marketing problems that exists.

At the same time, your reputation may paint you as a jovial, quick-witted conversationalist, or a fire-breathing control freak who always demands the last word.

Either way, in the minds of your colleagues, team members, and prospects—and even your friends and family members—it's the whole picture that comes to mind when they think of you. And that's a picture you have a lot of control in creating as your brand.

Your brand must include more than your competencies. You must not rely solely on your brain or work ethic. This is where the soft variable really matters.

If you were interviewing two candidates whose resumes were virtually identical and both were clearly competent and experienced, what would be the differentiators? Personality, people skills, communication, sense of humor?

Would you choose the know-it-all who pontificates and provides a litany of self-serving stories? Or would you prefer the good listener? Someone who's all business all the time or maybe someone with a great sense of humor?

For me, that's a no-brainer. How we present ourselves in our interactions, our posture, tone of voice, style, dress, gait, and manners are all part of the equation. Do we make excuses, or do we take responsibility for the people and events within our circle of influence? Do we respect others' time and space?

BRANDING YOURSELF

Personally, I have prided myself in being the person that can be counted on. I consider it my responsibility to see that my work is done correctly and delivered on time. My clients know that I will be honest with them; I tell them the truth, even if they are not going to like hearing it.

Plus, they can count on me for no surprises in our interactions and agreements. I have their backs and they have my full commitment. If I don't know the answer, I say so, but I also add that I will research until we find the answer or the right person to help.

In a world of ambiguity and inconsistencies, I have succeeded by keeping my promises, period. The funny thing is, doing what you say you are going to do sounds so normal, but it is not common. My clients know they can count on me to produce the results we agree to create, and this has worked for me from the time I was babysitting, mowing lawns, and taking over the extra shift as a waitress.

Your own branding strategy begins with you asking yourself what you want to be known for and writing it down in detail. Imagine you are looking for a candidate to fill your own executive role and research the internet to see who your competition is and what these people are doing.

LinkedIn profiles can be very helpful too. As you read them, ask yourself what you like or don't like about other executives' profiles, then tailor yours to reflect the image and qualities you want to be known for.

The next step is to determine who your client is and why they should use you versus other candidates for your role. Read reviews about your competitors. It is critical that you identify what makes you special or different from the other contenders in your area of expertise.

Ask yourself what you want to deliver and how you will deliver it. Make certain this is not only realistic, but that you are willing to commit to delivering it as promised. "As promised" is the key here, as you are only as good as your word in the eyes of the people you deal with.

Second chances are rarely given in business. Ask others for advice, have an open mind, and do your homework. Ask trusted friends, family, and associates for straight talk about you—both your strengths and your opportunities for improvement.

Last but not least, talk to a marketing expert to get another perspective on how to get the word out about you and your business. Do not limit yourself. Talk to everyone you know about your new business and how excited you are. You will generate interest, as well as make valuable contacts, by just talking with enthusiasm about your venture.

You can learn something from everyone just by listening—and you never know who knows whom.

When creating our own personal brand, we really need to know ourselves. Sometimes that means we have to ask others how they see us, which can be a revealing and challenging experience all in one! This is the beginning of determining your brand—what you want people to say about you, your service, and your expertise.

Just remember not to shoot the messenger when someone tells you their observations of what they see in your behavior. It's better to use simple, nonconfrontational questions to find out the reasons behind those opinions, and use the feedback you discover as a simple barometer of your success at communicating your brand.

If you like what you hear, how can you reinforce your brand image and take it to the next level? And if you don't like the feedback coming in, how can you adjust what you're putting out for people to latch onto as your image?

You need to be in charge of shaping what people say about you. Do not leave your legacy to chance.

KNOW YOUR BLIND SPOTS

I was assigned to work with a CEO of a major division of a Fortune 500 company. Apparently, a member of the highly valued, long-tenured executives had already resigned as a result of this CEO, who had been in this role for about seven months. There were many other disgruntled employees as well.

As is my policy with each new assignment, I interviewed the coaching candidate to determine if there was a good fit between us.

During my initial interview, I ask clients to tell me what is working, what is not working, what they consider pressing issues with their career and their staff or team, and what a typical day in the office is like. This individual began by telling me that he was very annoyed when an early-morning emergency meeting had been called the day before. In his opinion, nobody wanted to go to it and that meeting was a waste of time.

I suspected there was a little more to the story, so I probed by asking him to tell me everything that was said, where the meeting was held, and other details.

After lots of probing, I discovered that the CEO's first words to his staff on entering the boardroom were "Who the fuck called this meeting?" He honestly did not understand that his directness, profanity, and tone of voice scared the hell out of everyone!

In his defense, he told me he had never had a problem with his style before. I wondered why, and as it turned out, previous to his job as the corporation's chief executive, he had owned his own firm. And he had no interest in changing his behavior or leadership style now.

If someone is not interested in coaching, I don't waste anyone's money or time trying to "fix" them. So I scheduled a meeting with the executive team to discuss next steps.

Bottom line, this man was a brilliant strategist and visionary—he just wasn't a people person. I am happy to report that, as a result of our investigations and interventions, the organization soon created a position for this man that allowed them to capitalize on his skills. His new office was located in another building.

This gave the company several extra advantages too, since they would also retain valued employees, mitigate the risk of potential litigation, and avoid losing his talent to the competition.

CHAPTER 14

Getting That Interview

Want some good news?

Persistence pays off. That is a promise.

Whether you're trying to garner publicity for a cause you believe in, support for a program you're responsible for, or attention and consideration for a new role at your company, don't just apply for the position. Distinguish yourself in some way. Then get creative and don't give up.

Let me tell you about my first job interview. I had heard a rumor that there was an opening in the Oak Park School District, but it hadn't yet been officially announced. They were looking for an internal candidate, and the unofficial job board was just starting to pick up steam.

Understand that this was and remains a very prestigious school district and I really, really wanted this teaching opportunity. I knew I was well qualified and ready for it too.

When I called the superintendent's office to inquire about the position, the administrative assistant told me she could not schedule a meeting, as no open position had been announced.

From that day forward, I contacted the office every single day for thirty-four days. Every morning, I would make the call and try to schedule an interview.

Each day, the assistant listened patiently, responding with the official reply that there was nothing she could do. Finally, on the thirty-fourth day, she asked me, "If I get you an interview for the position, will you stop calling me?"

I'm happy to tell you, I got the interview and I got the job! In gratitude, I also brought a box of candy to the assistant for being such a doll.

Your choices determine your future and the quality of your life. Choose wisely.

I was gracious, warm, funny, and polite with each call. I never acted sarcastic or threatening. I never said, "I know there is a job and you are lying to me," or anything that was mean-spirited.

This is genuinely my style, and I love to make people laugh. I love to make fun of myself as well. This style has served me well my entire career.

What style will serve you well? This is one of the most important questions you will ever answer. Choose wisely, because this will be your reputation forever.

RAISE YOUR HAND, LADIES!

Self-awareness and how you carry yourself are critical to managing how people see you. It is not who you are but who people think you are that will determine your future success.

A number of prominent female CEOs I've worked with have identified a major problem that is directly affecting women's professional advancement to the corner office: the leadership ambition gap.

To put it simply, enculturation and learned patterns of behavior have created a feeling of insecurity among women on their way to the top. We have been conditioned to look at the glass ceiling, admire those who have cracked it, and then quietly walk away.

On the surface, social pressures related to work-life balance rise up to add stress, guilt, and self-doubt to our goals and accomplishments. Plus, many of us hold the mistaken belief that family and professional life are mutually exclusive.

But there is a deeper, more significant reason for the divide. It goes back to the lessons we learned by watching what others do, not what they say, about raising our hands.

Dr. Mark Jusczcak is a brilliant young man I have the privilege of mentoring. He is a true advocate for female executives, and he has done extensive research on the leadership ambition gap.

Mark and I are both big believers in teaching through stories. They are easy to remember and easy to pass along, and a well-told story gets to the essence of the problem. When we partner in presenting workshops together, Mark frequently tells this story to exemplify the power of what we have silently learned and retained.

IT DOESN'T MATTER HOW TALENTED YOU ARE IF NOBODY KNOWS YOU ARE THERE

When Mark was in sixth grade, two students were at the top of the class: Mike and Tatiana. Mike had virtually straight As with a 98% average.

Tatiana worked harder than Mike and maintained a 99.5% average for the year. She was, by all academic merits, the better student. She not only worked harder, she did more and achieved higher scores on the state and national exams.

As sixth grade rolled into seventh and eighth, the gap between Mike and Tatiana's grades grew slightly bigger. Mike's average slipped to 97.8% for the last two years of grammar school, and Tatiana's climbed to a 99.6%.

At the end of her senior year, however, Tatiana was stunned to discover that Mike had been declared valedictorian!

At first glance, the oversight seemed unbelievable to Tatiana. Everything on paper was in her favor, except for one thing: she never raised her hand. You see, in this school valedictorian was chosen based on a combination of grades and teacher recommendations.

Sure, during any single day of school, it wouldn't have mattered much if Mike's hand was in the air to answer a question and Tatiana's was down. But the cumulative effect of all the days during those years resulted in a small but significant perceptual difference—which cut Tatiana out of the spotlight at a crucial moment.

Overall, Mike simply raised his hand more, which meant that he was also called on more. As a result, Mike was perceived as being more proactive, more involved. And in the eyes of the teachers and the students around him, he was recognized as being smarter.

I can guess what you're thinking—it shouldn't matter. But it did for Tatiana. And that one self-conscious habit, possibly coerced because of peer pressure and inwardly accepted by Tatiana as polite, changed the results of her accomplishments, but not for the better.

While "raising your hand" is normally defined as a decision to participate, that is incorrect and incomplete. We are going to change that definition. To raise your hand doesn't mean to participate, it means to initiate.

Specifically, it means to initiate an action whereby your communicated thoughts can directly impact the world around you. What you do with those opportunities is your call, but you must do something!

In short, that's what leaders do: initiate. So raise your hand from day one. That is the only way you will find your voice and be heard.

FIND YOUR VOICE, OR SOMEONE ELSE GETS THE CREDIT

It is important to receive recognition for a great idea, a great performance, or a job well done. It sounds like a no-brainer, but all too often, women dismiss this notion as "bragging."

Perhaps this is a result of how we have been conditioned to let the men take the kudos. I don't know for sure, but I do see this tendency for women to sidestep claiming their due as often or as naturally as men do.

Don't get me wrong—I am not suggesting that you hog the credit and keep it for yourself, rather than sharing it with deserving members of your team. In my experience, great leaders are generous with sharing the acclaim (even if it was their idea that generated the win).

Remember, sharing accolades is different than letting someone else take the credit from you. Understand the distinction; it is very significant and powerful.

Speak up. Silence can be misunderstood as disinterest, disagreement, or worse. That's why it's important to find your voice, make your point, and make it clearly.

After all, if you do not claim the credit for things you have done, someone else will receive the benefits that should accrue to you. And you cannot find your voice by letting others take advantage of you.

Finding your voice is the vehicle by which you build your brand and reputation. Be generous with giving people recognition and sharing pats on the back appropriately, but make certain you receive acknowledgment for your hard work.

Of course, the flip side of the coin also applies here. Be sure to take ownership and responsibility when something doesn't pan out as you planned too. Your voice must be heard and perceived as an honest one.

Keep in mind, you are building a reputation of integrity and trust for the long term. And by your words and actions, you determine how your voice will be heard.

THE DIRTY DOZEN

There are many pitfalls on the way to building your reputation. Below are twelve mistakes that can ruin your professional image. Be sure to take stock of your own behavior and avoid these traps.

1. Showing off your knowledge. No one likes a know-it-all. While demonstrating your intelligence is great for a job interview, when working with your team, don't flaunt your smarts. Nobody cares!

2. Being negative. Find a way to reframe and share thoughts in a positive way. People avoid negative people.

3. Hogging the credit. Take the credit when and only when you've earned it. A team effort needs to be recognized as one. Share the credit or pay a price.

4. Failing to accept responsibility for mistakes. Shifting blame onto others breeds resentment. Just own it and move on.

5. Speaking up too often. You don't always need to always add your two cents.

6. Favoring some coworkers over others. Be careful of where you sit, how you talk, and whom you talk to. Everyone needs a fair shot.

7. Inability to apologize. Admit the mistake and move on!

8. Letting emotion into your communications. Emotions need not be in the equation when you are speaking in a business setting. Anger is not your friend at the office.

9. Keeping others in the dark. Failing to share information and being territorial will damage your reputation very quickly.

10. Speaking with sarcasm. In most cases, it hurts people, causes embarrassment, or offends someone.

11. Interrupting. Let people finish, even when they are wrong and you know the answer. Be kind and courteous at all costs.

12. Invading personal space. Be aware of keeping an appropriate distance from others and do not stand above someone else—it can be intimidating and just plain uncomfortable.

In the words of noted management guru and thought leader Marshall Goldsmith, "What got you

Fast Track to the Corner Office for Women

here won't get you there." His book is enlightening reading with tips on preparing for the next step in your career. While you may get away with some quirks, consistent bad behavior can prevent you from reaching your personal and professional goals.

Remember, as a top-level executive, you're in the relationship business. Continuing to drop tiny "relationship bombs" tends to create negative perceptions that can hold any person or executive back.

This is especially true for women, since we're held to a different standard. There's no room for "almost." Women need to go full throttle in ALL aspects of relationship management to establish their credibility among peers and beyond.

One major theme in Goldsmith's advice is knowing when to speak up—and when not to. Often it's more important to listen to what others have to say than it is to share your own thoughts. Furthermore, when you do speak, remember to keep in mind the image you are projecting. Negativity, complaints, and snarky comments are seldom welcome, and can paint you as someone who isn't interested in finding solutions.

Another source of relationship problems is failure to respect your colleagues and an exaggerated view of yourself. While self-promotion is necessary to a point, overselling yourself is as damaging to your reputation as underselling. Take a clear view of your accomplishments and value, and while you shouldn't shy away from owning your successes, you need not flaunt them at every opportunity.

Also take care to recognize your team for their contributions. People are more willing to give you more of their effort if they know they will be appreciated for it. Show your coworkers you see their dedication by thanking them privately and recognizing them publicly for their work. Treat them with fairness and respect, and they will support you when you need it.

On the flip side, it is just as important to take responsibility and own your mistakes as it is to give praise where it's due. Deflecting blame onto coworkers can destroy relationships and erase trust. While no one is happy to have a problem laid at their feet, dealing with every incident with decorum, a cool head, and a proactive outlook will gain you respect and trust among your colleagues.

For more of Goldsmith's advice on how to avoid "transactional flaws" in business relationships, I highly recommend his book, *What Got You Here Won't Get You There*.

CHAPTER 15

Connection is the Currency of Relationships

Want to know the key to creating sustainable success and relationships that work?

Establishing a real connection with someone is very different than communicating with them. The difference is so significant, I cannot overemphasize this point.

For example, why do you make a purchase from one person over another, if they are selling the exact same product? Because there is a connection. They remind you of someone you like, or they make you laugh or smile. They make you feel something pleasant.

Maybe it is the way they look you in the eye, touch your hand or reach your heart with a story they tell, but make no mistake, a connection has been made.

We all know the importance of top-notch communication skills, both written and verbal. However, connecting takes this to a whole different level. Don't believe me? Then try a little experiment.

The next time you're in a crowded lobby, a busy streetscape, or even a boardroom presentation where you're meeting colleagues for the first time, watch the different reactions when you smile at a stranger rather than just looking at them. Smiles and happiness are indeed contagious.

So, if you want to be successful and happy, the solution is actually quite simple. Just smile, laugh, and enjoy the things you're doing. Pretty soon, you'll find that others will want to be around you.

Now picture the opposite example. We all have met people that we want to avoid. In fact, if we see them walking down the hall, we might duck into the washroom or change direction. Why? Because they are negative, and they are likely going to complain and share their grief if you give them half a chance.

Notice how, in polite conversation, most people ask, "How are you?" I know that with negative people, I am always sorry I have asked that question. Because it seems to open the floodgates and I am going to hear everything that is wrong or not going well. Sometimes I wish I could bite my own tongue off when I casually ask these people "How are you?"

Then you have the other side of the coin—people who always find the good in any relationship or event and are generally positive. They rarely burden anyone with their distress. Instead, they are a pleasure to greet and we enjoy interacting and sharing our experiences.

Long ago, I realized the real value of caller ID as a tool to help me maintain my positive outlook on a day-to-day basis. For me, caller ID helps me to avoid the negative, draining few that are toxic even just to listen to.

This is especially true when, as sometimes happens, we love them, are related to them, or must deal with them as a result of other agreements or obligations, but that doesn't mean it must be on their timetable or in the way they demand.

For example, I like to return calls to difficult people when I know they are unavailable, so I can answer them without being sucked into their drama and misery.

Work on connecting, as the currency of relationships is invaluable. When we like someone or enjoy being around them, we tend to get the best results more easily and more often. I'm sure you prefer to listen and share with positive people. After all, we all have more than enough stress, crime, deadlines, and drama going on around us—no need to contribute to that ever-full fountain!

Instead, try a little tenderness, compassion, understanding, kindness, and humor. You'll find the world becomes a pleasant place to build your career and your life.

I know we don't have any control over how others behave, but you do have a choice as to your own behavior, as well as the subsequent perception that you create about yourself. This perception is a large part of your brand, and you must determine early on what you want others to see and say about you.

People are always saying something about others, even if it is with a pause or a wordless reply. For example, if I ask someone if they know so-and-so, they might say I don't know if it's someone they've never met. If they don't like the person I've asked about, they will hesitate or pause. But if they like the person they immediately respond with a yes!

Just because someone doesn't verbally say yuck, ick, or "That person is nasty," it doesn't mean they haven't conveyed something. Body language is so telling!

How do you want to leave people feeling? I know that I want people to smile when they hear my name. If your reputation is that you are smart or capable, that is nice, but not enough. If you are smart, capable, and very nice, you are way ahead of the game. After all, since we spend more of our waking hours at work then we do at home, doesn't it make sense to benefit from being around people that are pleasant and positive? Even better, doesn't it make sense to be one of those people yourself?

Life is hard enough. We don't need to make it tougher than it already is by acting disgruntled, obstructive, or negative. Laugh, play, and make the most of things—and don't forget to laugh at yourself.

Let people into your world as a person, even just a little, and they'll respond in kind. This is all about connecting. It always has been and always will be.

CLEAR COMMUNICATION

Let's take connecting to the next level with a short story about the talented young executive I was coaching a few years ago who was on the fast track at the corporation where he worked. This young man was taking his executive development seriously.

As you're undoubtedly aware, executive development covers a wide range of skills and abilities. One of the topics I'm frequently asked to guide my clients on is how to conduct productive meetings. In this executive's case, I provided him with a one-page document on effective meetings with one of the bullet points emphasizing the importance of time management.

This young man was progressing very well, picking up the finer points of starting and ending a meeting on time, keeping to the agenda, and reading your audience. He had been building rapport and relationships with ease and was genuinely well-liked.

However, I heard some rumblings that people hated attending his meetings. Hate is a very strong word, but I soon discovered why everyone dreaded his team meetings. As I customarily do when I'm coaching someone, I asked him to arrange for me to sit in on a meeting in real time. As I approached the meeting room later that morning, he was standing by the door greeting people with a smile.

Following my bulleted list almost to the letter, he had sent out an agenda in advance. He provided beverages and snacks on the table. I couldn't help thinking to myself, "How bad could this meeting be?"

Right on time, the meeting started with a warm welcome and the executive displayed the meeting agenda and objectives in a PowerPoint slideshow for all to see. He was off to a great start.

Until he brought out the stopwatch.

As he went around the table and asked each person to present their data, he would start the watch. Each person was given precisely three minutes to say their piece and not one second more.

Needless to say, there were no questions answered and no dialogue among the team members. Everyone was anxious and frustrated. It was similar to taking a test in college with those rigid start/stop directions for everyone to dread. In fact, the executive would say "Stop," and his team members could not continue to present or answer.

Now I understood firsthand why people did not want to attend his meetings!

At the end of the session, he proudly announced that the meeting was a success, as it had ended on time. In effect, this was great example of someone taking a point very literally. It was a classic case of letter of the law versus intent!

I spent the next hour explaining the value of dialogue among the team, the importance of questions, and how the inclusion of non-agenda items can be invaluable. I also wanted him to understand that his team needed opportunities to connect with one another, to become comfortable and build rapport and camaraderie with one another as people. He soon realized that in to the interest of staying on time, he was sacrificing the relationships and exchanges so vital to a productive meeting.

The good news is, he understood as I explained the difference and he learned how to conduct a productive meeting where people shared, contributed, and participated fully. His team was eternally grateful.

Since then, I am now even more careful to double check my client's understanding and interpretation of what I am asking for or suggesting.

As the saying goes, it's not what you say, it's what they hear!

CHAPTER 16

A Surprising Connection

Now that you've reached the end of *Fast Track to the Corner Office for Women,* you deserve congratulations and recognition for making your way through the surprisingly intricate web of events, strategies, and details that continue to have the greatest effects on my career.

More importantly, I hope I've been effective at boiling those events and observations down to their core lessons for you, so you can use the wisdom I've gained through my own experiences, guided by the business and life experiences of the mentors I've had the good fortune to know.

My hope for you is that you'll take what you need and use what works to reach the next pinnacle in your own career—and the next one, and the next one, and the one after that.

As the career trajectories of the hundreds of executives I've coached and mentored throughout these thirty-plus years have shown, you can do this too.

Like you, they've all had astounding goals to strive for, along with obstacles that seemed to be equally astonishing. And yet, with a handful of effective skillsets, their unique talents, and the right mindset, we've all seen the difference they're making on the job and in the world at large.

Their paths got clearer once they figured out the reality—that nobody does it alone.

As I was putting this book together, a group of surprising connections started to appear right before my eyes. And even with all of the people I've met, the deals I've put in place, and the mentors I've known, I hadn't quite realized them all until just now.

You rarely see it as it happens. But looking back on things, now I'm making all these connections as if they're brand new.

Do you remember my story behind the last go-cart victory of my racing career when I appeared in front of all those people as the woman in the pack who won the New York World's Fair Cart Classic?

Well, I couldn't know it at the time, but it turns out that Bernice and Sascha—two of the ladies I ended up enjoying lifelong connections, friendships, and mentorships with—were actually at that event too!

Of course, I didn't know them yet and they didn't know me. But they were all right there with their kids when I won that race. And their boys, of course, wished that they had been racing too.

It stood out that a young woman had won. And I was that woman.

It's not surprising that my mentors-to-be were at the New York World's Fair. But the funny part was, their kids were hounding them, "We wanna race go-carts!" and their mothers were saying, "You're not racing!" And there I was, the girl who won it.

I think that really goes to show you, there's a reason that we draw people into our lives, and we get to know them. We're all working things out.

You never know where things will lead and you never know who else is watching when you reach a milestone, suffer a defeat, or win an award.

So do your best to show up as the person you intend to be. Get good, get resourceful, and get noticed for it. Be sure to stick with something long enough to master it and you'll be fine.

And remember, above all, you can do this too. If I can do this, you can do this—I'm not some genius! But I also didn't wait for things to happen or wait for my mentors to come over and talk to me. I went over and introduced myself.

I don't know if they would have come to me. They probably wouldn't have—why would they? But they received me because they understood that I was asking them for help. They liked that and they got it.

After all, what's the worst that can happen? Nothing!

Just promise me you won't let "nothing" be the result you settle for. You're a woman—the most capable, resourceful, and astonishing being on the planet.

Let's show them what you can do!

Dr. Betty O

Dr. Betty Orlandino, PhD

Dr. Betty Orlandino, PhD, is a certified talent consultant and Master Performance Coach and mentor based in Boca Raton, Florida.

Fresh out of high school, "Fast Betty" was the first woman ever offered a driving position in Formula One racing in 1968. For more than thirty years, she's been working directly with high-potential women, celebrities, and C-suite executives at Fortune 100 and Fortune 500 corporations across the United States, including Navistar, Federated/Macy's Department Stores, USG Corporation, Kohler Company, and US Foods, to name a few.

In her coaching and everything she does, Dr. Betty O brings her indelible warmth, good humor, and a family-sized helping of the kick-ass "Chicago chutzpah" she grew up with. That's why she's been featured by media outlets including *Time* magazine, *USA Today*, the *New York Times*, the *Chicago Sun-Times*, and the *Wall Street Journal*. She has also appeared on local and national radio and television broadcast networks, including NBC, ABC, and CBS. You can find more info on her website at www.drbettyo.com.

Dr. Betty O's mantra is "Go to school on everyone. It's free, and worst case, you'll learn what not to do!" And always remember that nobody does it alone.

Acknowledgments

If I wanted to shine a light on the many people who contributed to this book through our life experiences together, I could barely scratch the surface of the gratitude I feel toward them all. But this short list of names represents those people who have left an indelible mark on my life through the years. I hope each of you knows how much of a difference you've made.

Lieutenant Helen M. Weber, my mom, whose courage, determination, work ethic, and example put me on the right track from the get-go.

My daughter Jacki. Unbeknownst to her, she was the motivation for me to be the best I could be, so that she would be proud of me too. I worked full time, attended graduate school, studied, and burned the candle at both ends. And as I'd fall asleep at the kitchen table where I studied, I would shake myself awake and remind myself I had a daughter to raise and provide for. I could do anything, knowing she was watching. I am so proud of Jacki's accomplishments, both academically and professionally, as her uncompromising high standards and unwavering integrity are key ingredients to her success as a woman, wife, daughter, and forensic scientist.

Professor Beulah Drom, who provided practical advice, unwavering encouragement, and common sense, and for thirty-three years, taught me the value of asking questions.

Sascha, who provided a perspective I could have never imagined. Her relentless nudging (hammering), as she pushed me to grow and stretch out of my comfort zone, proved to be as invaluable as it was unforgettable. She kept me ahead of the curve and taught me to anticipate the unexpected by looking ahead and being prepared.

Dr. Marilyn Jacobson, for her generosity in mentoring me on business academics, and for being a superb resource and an exceptional associate.

Senator Bernard Neistein, who coached me on the real world–the good, the bad, and the ugly. The senator spent countless hours (seven years' worth), educating me on negotiations and politics, and provided me with so many incomparable introductions.

Last but not least, Bernice Pink, who brought me into her world, resulting in a great boost to my self-confidence and self-esteem when I needed it the most. Plus, she gave me a look at the behind-the-scenes world of the successful, wealthy, and privileged. In addition to teaching me social graces and the power of connection and relationships, she opened my eyes to the importance of perception. I'll never forget the worldly wisdom in Bernice's urging: "Don't leave it to chance; you are judged by your associations–whether you like it or not."

By example, Bernice helped me to appreciate what I have, and helped me realize that we must give back to our community and society at large. This is non-negotiable if you want to be happy and successful. Thank you, Bernice, for believing in me, encouraging me, and forcing me to examine things I did not want to look at. Rest in peace, my dear friend.

55535705R00072

Made in the USA
Columbia, SC
19 April 2019